ADVENTURES
OF THE HEBE

ADVENTURES OF THE HEBE

SAILING ON BRITAIN'S CANALS BETWEEN THE WARS

FROM THE ORIGINAL BOOKS BY DESMOND STOKER

EDITED BY SIMON STOKER

AMBERLEY

This book is dedicated to the memory of my son

DAVID STOKER
1979 – 2010

Yet if you should forget me for a while
And afterwards remember, do not grieve:
For if the darkness and corruption leave
A vestige of the thoughts that once I had,
Better by far you should forget and smile
Than you should remember and be sad.

Christina Rosetti

First published 2011

Amberley Publishing
Cirencester Road, Chalford
Stroud, Gloucestershire, GL6 8PE

www.amberleybooks.com

Copyright © Simon Stoker, 2011

The right of Simon Stoker to be identified as the Author
of this work has been asserted in accordance with the
Copyrights, Designs and Patents Act 1988.

British Library Cataloguing in Publication Data.
A catalogue record for this book is available from the British Library.

ISBN 978-1-4456-0221-9

Typesetting and Origination by Amberley Publishing.
Printed in Great Britain.

Contents

L&NWR railway pass from 1922 in the name of Stephen Stoker (see Plate 1).

Preamble

It is an age ago now, a different world in the decade before the Second World War. One without the sort of mass entertainment we now take for granted. A world without the internet, mobile telephones and 'celebrities' famous for being famous.

There was the good old steam radio, the programme changed perhaps twice a week at the local picture house, and that was about it. In the late 1920s and early 1930s you made mostly your own entertainment.

At that time my father, Desmond Stoker,[1] was in the midst of his medical studies at Edinburgh University (he would qualify as a doctor in 1933). During the long summers he was still an enthusiastic participant in his family's boating holidays around the canals and rivers of England. What made these holidays so different was that his father (my grandfather) Stephen was the owner of a fine double-skulling skiff named the *Hebe*[2] to which he had fitted sails and constructed a hooped frame to carry an awning for overnight accommodation. Food, utensils, clothing and other necessities were carefully stored about the boat.

The three Adventures recorded here cover over 700 miles and more than 300 locks, the last trip being the most ambitious with 300 miles and nearly 200 locks alone.

My grandfather, 'Pop' as he was known, was a railwayman. According to my father he started at the lowest level counting railway trucks and worked his way through the hierarchy of the London & North Western Railway to become Superintendent. He began rowing or sailing the canals probably before 1900.

Nearing retirement by the time these books were written, he elected to stay in Manchester rather than take a promotion to Swansea. At the time he was responsible, my father relates, for the railway 'from Crewe to Carlisle and

---

1. Only his mother ever called him by his first name, Arthur. To the rest of the world he was always known as Desmond, although I have always used his full initials – ADS.
2. Hebe was the Goddess of Youth, daughter of Zeus and Hera, who served nectar and ambrosia to assorted other gods and goddesses on Mount Olympus.

from Liverpool to Hull'. The family lived in Stockport, and so *Hebe* was kept on the Macclesfield Canal (hence her 'home port' of High Lane).

Pop eventually retired to Evesham and my only real memories of him are from the viewpoint of a very small boy in the early 1950s. To me, then, he was a rotund, white-haired old man with a rattly Morris 8 who grew asparagus in his garden.

My father eventually owned, consecutively, three narrowboats. A 'Stour lifter' butty called *Stoke*; a wonderful Bridgewater butty called *Loretto*, which had been converted to a motor with a sweeping counter to her butty rudder and was, in my opinion, the best narrowboat I ever steered; and the *Rea*, an old tar boat bought from someone on the Peak Forest Canal, with a lumpy and noisy National diesel as its power unit. He eventually developed his own design of Dexion angle-iron and marine ply and had it built at Tom Trevethick's yard in Nottingham. ('It'll never float, Doctor!'). This started at 32 feet but was unbolted and extended to 48 feet because my mother complained she had not enough room after three narrowboats. Note the increase is in multiples of 8 feet – the length of a sheet of ply.

But this is to race ahead a little too far. In 1928, 1929 and 1930 the world was a very different place. Teenagers were certainly not all-knowing gadget-carriers unable to communicate without some form of microchip. My father was nineteen years old when he recorded the first Adventure, and to a modern reader his style might seem florid and naive, but it also reflects that inter-war period of relative simplicity and of family, where such things as a peaceful Sunday morning would be noted by the loudness of a cuckoo's song or the noise of a grasshopper.

I have no intention of judging such matters. Whatever my father's style, these Adventures pre-date some of the greater writers and observers of the time. I have not rewritten his text in any way, save the occasional edit for clarity, for I have no wish to spoil his stories. The one-way glass of history now makes such Adventures a snapshot of England at that time, so my contribution is to try to set each year in its historical context with a few facts and figures to set the scene, especially for younger readers. The footnotes throughout the text and the appendices at the end are my own.

Most of the pictures in this book are reproduced either from my father's original prints or, where possible, from his original 4' x 3' glass negatives of the time. All other postcards and reproductions are credited as such.

More than eighty years after the events recorded here, I hope he would approve.

SSS
2011

Author's Preface

It is in no apologetic spirit that I offer this small work for your contemplation, or if you go further than that for your perusal. Maybe it is 'a poor thing but it is mine own'. If, dear reader, it meets not with your approval then shut the book and never mind it.

I was not paid to write it, neither having written it do I expect to sell it, and therefore I was able to please myself as to its ultimate form.

In fact it was more to provide a souvenir for myself in future years of the happy days spent on this voyage than to tell others of them. Indeed, what may appear to you to be just an ordinary sentence will bring to my mind half-a-score of associations meant for my thoughts alone and would, if communicated to you, appear only as a senseless jumble.

Therefore I reiterate, I do not apologise as is the fashion nowadays, neither on the one hand do I implore you to peruse the book. If, after having read thus far, you do not like it then shut it, but if perchance it appeals to your imagination then do the obvious thing and read it to the end.

I am,
Your humble servant,

ADS

Edinburgh, 1928

HISTORICAL MISCELLANY
1928

6 January	The River Thames floods parts of London. Fourteen people are drowned.
February	Great Britain and Northern Ireland compete at the Winter Olympics in St Moritz, winning one bronze medal.
12 March	Malta becomes a British Dominion.
26 April	Madame Tussaud's opens in London.
28 September	The first 'talkie' film is shown in Britain.
30 September	Alexander Fleming discovers penicillin.
18 November	Walt Disney's *Steamboat Willie* features Mickey Mouse in sound.

ALSO:

The BBC (formerly 2LO) is only a year old (established on 1 January 1927).

Haile Selassie is crowned King of Abassinia.

D. H. Lawrence writes *Lady Chatterley's Lover*.

Ravel composes *Bolero*.

The weather was notably wet across England and Wales. A north to north-westerly severe gale produced a strong surge down the North Sea coast of eastern England which combined with a high ('spring') tide in the Thames estuary, causing severe flooding in the London area as the Embankment was breached in several places with many roads damaged. The second half of November 1928 was notably stormy. It was one of the severest winters of the twentieth century (up to 1939/40).

BOOK ONE
THE WANDERINGS OF THE HEBE
1928

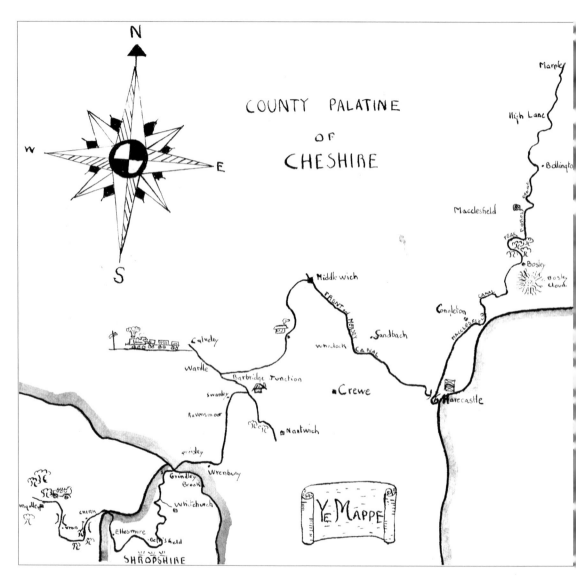

Original hand–drawn map (see Plate 2).

Chapter I

The Hebe – The Crew – The Start – Cheshire

It might perhaps be as well to begin by explaining that this is not a treatise concerning a certain regrettable Greek goddess well known to the ancients, but an account of a pleasure cruise on inland waterways. Or, as a lady on a barge[1] who is by way of becoming an intimate friend of the Gunner's once remarked, the tale of a fortnight's jackcraft. Jackcraft is the term applied by true citizens of the canals to the art of voyaging to the danger of life and limb in 'cockboats'.

Our craft, the *Hebe*, is a two-paired in-rigged sculling boat, to which the Commander and the Gunner have added various sails. In conforming to the conditions of the canal the rig has become unorthodox, but nevertheless the two aforementioned members of the crew are ready to back the *Hebe* against any sailing boat on the canal.

The crew consists of, in order of importance, the Commander – a stout fellow well versed in canal usage and guaranteed to be able to converse with a heated bargee yet hold his own withal. The Stewardess, to whom the provision of plenty of coats is very important, but one who can boil an egg with the best. The Powder Monkey, who loves not the weary oar but who has a delight in doing nothing, excepting, perhaps, reading a novel or disporting in the watery element. And the Gunner who, like the Commander, is conversant with the etiquette of the canal. He delights in turning locks and when on the canal does as the canal does. There is in him a mixture of inland canal usage and sea custom which leads, or rather urges, him to do all manner of things in order to (as he himself says with a nautical hitch to his belt) have all shipshape and Bristol fashion.

---

1. Through most of the books ADS refers to 'barges' when for most of the time he means narrowboats. (In later life he would have been horrified to have used such a term!)

Clockwise from left: The Commander, the Gunner (ADS), the Stewardess and the Powder Monkey.

For instance, he spends hours coiling every rope in the boat into great round target-like coils, and as far as lock-keys go they are the darlings of his heart. He is also at times most conscientious in the upkeep of his log to which, all other sources of information having failed, the other members of the crew will refer.

According to this log we apparently 'cast off at 3 pm' on Friday 10th August. It was against all tradition and superstition to sail on a Friday, but we were in such a hurry and anxiety to get to the wide open spaces – where men are, well, bargees – that we did not trouble to consult any oracle as to whether the day was propitious or not.

The Clerk of the Weather must have admired our temerity and Old Sol shone his best for our benefit. The countryside was looking beautifully fresh, a gentle zephyr moved the trees from time to time and caused a rustle in the corn fields, altogether delightful both to eye and ear.

We had not progressed very far before we had to make a halt. We had not forgotten anything but the inner man was taking account of the fresh air and politely informing us – against our better judgement – that it was time for tea. There being no time like the present, and no bank quite so soft and shady as the one we were passing at that moment, we hove to and indulged our appetites. Having been refreshed and rested we set forth at about 5.30 towards Bosley.

The country at one side of the canal differed vastly from that on the other. To one side on the whole length of the canal the vast Cheshire Plain stretches out as flat as a pancake, right away into the blue distance, where on a very clear day one can distinguish a faint purple line alleged by knowing ones to

Near Pott Shrigley.

be the Welsh mountains. On the other side the eye goes no further than a few miles, for rising abruptly from the canal's edge the hills of Derbyshire line the horizon.

What a contrast. Cheshire was a carpet of trees, of beautiful lush green fields and great wild scrambling thick rose-covered hedgerows. Cottages peeped out here and there, black and white with thick walls leaning at many different angles and roofed with a stout brown thatch. A rambler rose, as often as not, crept up the wall and climbed over the porch in which Age could be seen playing with Youth.

On the other side rose the hills of Derbyshire, bleak and cold. Only a few trees clung tenaciously to the bottom of a valley or ventured timidly up a slope. The fields were peopled with sheep which fed on the short dry grass so different from the sweet-smelling hay and flowers of Cheshire. Instead of blossoming hedgerows, dry-stone walls intersected and ran without a break, excepting a gate now and then, for miles and miles. The houses were not the agreeable crazy black and white affairs of the plain, but solid stone and roofed with cold blue slate. The effect altogether on one's mind as one voyages along is pretty much what one might feel on crossing the Styx. On one side the country is warm, comfortable and lazy, on the other it is dark and cold and energetic-looking.

We soon passed Bollington, down in the vale, surrounded by hills and making believe with the aid of a couple of mills to be industrious. Above Bollington, at the top of a long steep slope, there rises a whitewashed conical stone structure known as White Nancy. The exact purpose of White Nancy

The Powder Monkey bow-hauling near Bollington.

The *Hebe* near
'Royal Oak'.

is unknown. Some say it is an old witches' temple, others that it is merely the highest point in Cheshire. It is doubtful whether White Nancy really *is* in Cheshire.

So the erection remained to us a mystery; a suspicious building not to be thought of at night, but giving an agreeable thrill nevertheless when spoken of in connection with witches and dead men's spirits.

In this part of the world there is great interest taken in fishing. Anglers turn out by the hundred for the competitions of a Saturday afternoon or a Sunday. The mania cannot be very well accounted for; it is not as though any fish worth catching were to be had. Indeed, in a competition held lately the winner had only 17 oz, and to make up this weight he had about 18 fish.

At Macclesfield, which place we passed at about 8 o'clock, we were continually passing hordes of juvenile fishers. The Commander said it was all very sad. Nobody minded an old man recounting the size of the fish that just got away the other week, but if tender infants were going to take it up he felt something ought to be done about it.

Soon after passing Macclesfield we hove to for the night near a little village whose name we could not discover, and which accordingly has to go by the name of 'Royal Oak'.

Chapter II

Beseiged by cows – The swing bridge – Bosley Cloud –
Bredon Hill – Newly tarred lock beams –
Annoying old man – Church Lawton

SATURDAY 11TH AUGUST

The Commander and the Gunner were awakened early by a violent shaking
of their tent. First one corner would shake, then the poles would tremble and
the whole caboodle looked as though it were about to fall on the inmates
and smother them. The Commander accordingly rose in great wrath to
investigate the cause of this disturbance. He found it to be an amiable crowd
of heifers, curious as to the queer structure which had grown up in their
field overnight. They were engaged in tripping over the guy ropes to the
imminent danger of the tent.

Seizing a small bush the Commander laid about him and soon drove all but
one or two tardy beasts to a distance. In order to hasten the departure of one
of these latter he attempted to switch it over the snout. The animal merely
took this as an invitation to breakfast and proceeded with gusto to eat the
Commander's small arms.

Having returned from these cowboy exploits the Commander, with the
Gunner's help, proceeded to prepare breakfast, and afterwards with everything
packed away to the Gunner's satisfaction we pulled away and in a very few
minutes passed the Royal Oak where water was obtained.

There is a swing bridge at the Royal Oak about which the Commander
told us a story. It appeared that once in company with his friend R— and the
Gunner he had passed through this same bridge. The friend, R—, landed in
order to swing the bridge and clear the canal for the boat. Instead of standing

on the bridge and then pushing on the bank, or standing on the bank and pushing the bridge, R— stood on the bridge and pushed at the bridge. Of course it did not move. R— could not be made to understand why the bridge would not swing.

From here to Bosley the scenery changes somewhat. The canal is broad and there is that delightful look of flatness and placidity about the water which is not felt once in fifty times elsewhere. On the left rose up a very steep tall bank covered in undergrowth. The numerous old trees growing on the bank overarched and made a fine roof.

At the other side was the towpath bordered by a thick hedgerow through which at times could be obtained glimpses of Cheshire bathed in dew and sparkling in the morning sunlight. Here and there along the canal clumps and stretches of reeds stood up in the water. Except for an occasional water-hen, and sometimes a Kingfisher, there was no sign of life, while over everything an enchanting atmosphere of peace seemed to brood.

At about 9.30 we emerged from this leafy tunnel and soon after reached Bosley Top Lock and could see Bosley Cloud. This is a steep but rounded mountain, or rather a high hill standing in relation to the county around very much as Bredon stands in relation to the Vale of Evesham.

When going up the River Avon, Bredon Hill seems to march with you. You hire a boat at Tewkesbury and row upstream admiring the hill all day. The next day you wake up and see Bredon Hill as large as life just across the next field. You say to yourself, 'Well there's that adjectival hill again, we really must do a few miles today.'

Accordingly sleeves are rolled up, stretchers adjusted, and you settle down for a really good day's rowing. Then, in the evening, just as you are congratulating yourself on having lost it, you round a corner of the river and wreck the boat on a lump of Bredon Hill. That is what it is like all the way to Evesham. When people who don't know go up that river for the first time they think it all a nightmare and in a minute someone will shout '8 o'clock mister, hurry up or you'll miss the train.'

That is how it is with the Cloud. For miles you think you are leaving it behind and then, blam, you are almost crawling up the side of it.

The twelve locks at Bosley had been newly tarred and the Gunner's trousers after passing the boat down were newly tarred as well. Hearing the Stewardess remarking something about grease fetching it off, he seized the pot containing the rowlock grease and vigorously applied the same. Then by rubbing off the grease the tar was found to have come off also.

We descended the last lock at about 11.30 and a mile or so further on a halt was made for dinner. About two hours later we packed up and pulled away.

The Stewardess officiating at a Bosley lock.

As we progressed we passed a fine old country house. It stood four-square in a typical English park, the front facing the water with a green lawn sweeping down from a terrace to the canal which hereabouts broadened into a wide pool edged with water lillies over which the coots scuttled at our approach. The whole scene looked very fine, although the house appeared deserted, for the only sign of life was a Shetland pony which raised its head and pricked its ears in curiosity as we passed. We later learned this was Handel Hall, owned by a gentleman called Haddock.

At Hall Green – the terminus of the Macclesfield canal – we descended a lock with a drop of only nine inches and now that we had reached foreign waters we decided to celebrate the event and soon had spread the festive board.

A little further on we entered Plant's Lock and so started to descend a flight of 29, at the third of which we met two personages. One, a fat man with a red face, was merely making certain of the legality of our presence. It was the other with whom we had the most dealings. He was an oldish man who made the first advances by borrowing the Gunner's windlass and kindly drawing one set of paddles. Now while the lock was being filled he approached the Gunner and commented upon the state of the windlass. The eye was badly worn, the handle was small. In fact it was altogether a very dangerous instrument. It would fly off a pinion and maim for life, if not kill someone outright.

He had known many a young fellow cut off in his prime, all through having a worn windlass. The moral of the tale was that he himself had a windlass for sale. A beautiful windlass. It would fit any lock in the United Kingdom and the eye was not in the least bit worn. In fact it was such an excellent windlass that it would almost turn a lock by itself. Although to part with it would almost break his heart, in compassion for the Gunner he was willing to part with it for a certain sum. The Gunner, who has lived in Scotland, was not having any, and remarking that his present windlass had served him for some years he hitched nautically his trousers and trudged off to the next lock leaving the old man dumbfounded.

We now discovered that the last convoy of barges to be towed through Harecastle Tunnel had just gone down the locks and so they were all against us.[1] At the third lock, however, we met a Good Samaritan who, in consideration of our ready acquiescence in the matter of *pourboire*, and as he himself was going on foot as far as number twelve, offered to go ahead and prepare the locks for us.

We eagerly accepted his offer, and about a mile or so beyond Church Lawton, where the Gunner met several bargees whom he knew and who relieved us of work for a few locks, we pitched camp about 8 o'clock.

---

1. The top gates on the Trent and Mersey Canal are invariably single, unlike those on the Macclesfield Canal which are built as pairs (see page 59). This makes the Macclesfield gates appear delicate and attractive compared to the more common and clumsier variety, and it also gives an advantage in that when operating short-handed it is possible to open one side and hop from the open gate onto the still closed gate, saving a run around the whole length of the lock.

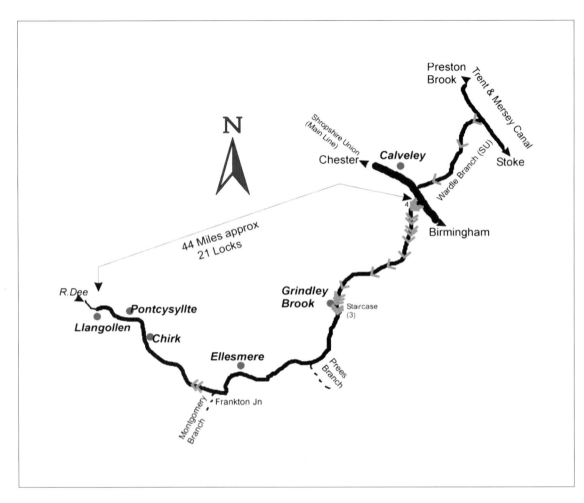

The Wardle Branch and the 'Welsh Canal'.

Chapter III

Watching the time and seizing the opportunity –
Natives of Middlewich – The Shropshire Union –
Ascending locks – Trustful nature of a hen keeper –
Church Minshull

SUNDAY 12TH AUGUST[1]

We were awakened by the pretty sound of the bells at Church Lawton. This delightful noise came echoing and ringing across the countryside in that charming manner possessed only by church bells in the country. As if in complete sympathy with the bells, the sun shone his best and was soon repairing the damage done by the previous night's rain.

We did not make a start immediately after breakfast for two reasons. The first was put forward gently by the Commander and the Gunner: 'We must wait until the boat cover dries. Couldn't possibly pack it wet you know'. The second was not advanced by them but nevertheless was the true reason for the delay. They knew that since last night's convoy had gone down the locks that no barge had passed and, consequently, all the locks would be against the *Hebe*. Therefore they wished to wait and see if possibly some boat would come up and thus relieve them of a lot of work.

Accordingly when, at about 10 a.m., two barges glided by there was great haste to pack up and get away. We gradually put the locks behind us, but as the day was beautifully fine we only drifted along slowly. There was not enough wind to flicker a candle flame and so we were reduced to rowing and towing.

Middlewich was approached late in the afternoon. About two locks before the town a party of youngsters started to follow us. Now, the Commander

---

1. 12 August was ADS's birthday. He would have been nineteen years old in 1928.

has a little way with juveniles. In this case he posed as the ignorant foreigner anxious to obtain as much information as possible regarding this town. Middlewich, he was informed, was quite a big town. In the course of the conversation he let drop an inquiry concerning Manchester.

Manchester is apparently situated in the north-east corner of England. It is a fairly big city, why it is almost twice as big as Middlewich – this in a tone implying that it really *was* big. 'Ay, it even had trams, you understand, Manchester has got trams.' Marvellous! Wonderful! Annus Mirabilis!

A little time after this encounter with the natives we descended the last two locks of the twenty-nine and turned at right-angles into the Shropshire Union Canal.[2] Hitherto the *Hebe* had descended all the locks we met. From now to Llangollen all the locks would be ascended. It was the job of the Stewardess and the Powder Monkey to remain in the boat and endeavour to save our varnish from being deposited on the walls of a lock. Now, as we had always come downwards, they had begun to regard locks as quite pleasant affairs in which *Hebe* was gently lowered. Thus they received somewhat of a shock when the boat was turned into the Wardle Branch and ascended.

The Commander and Gunner had foreseen this and had been chuckling to each other, anticipating the joke for the last five miles. The *Hebe* was manoeuvred into the lock and the gates shut with a bang as the Gunner drew the first of the underwater paddles. Now water began to burst in from below in great green bubbles. The Commander now drew the second ground paddle and water again rushed in from the side, further disturbing the placid lock. The Stewardess and Powder Monkey were alarmed. To crown it all the Gunner drew the third paddle situated high up in the lock gate and water poured in like two Niagras. This was the last straw and the Commander had to go to their aid. In fact it wasn't until near the end of the trip that these two overcame their horror of ascending locks.

After this little incident we proceeded to refresh the inner man and took a dish of tea about two miles further on.

Passing on our way we soon came to another lock with a pretty lockhouse. It had a beautiful garden and a charming little arch over the gate. In fact the Stewardess, taken with the look of the place, spent about fifteen minutes chatting with Mrs the lock keeper's wife, who was kind enough to fill our can with water. Not long after this we put up for the night as the sky looked threatening.

---

2. The Wardle Branch links the Shropshire Union main line and the Trent and Mersey Canal. It is ten miles long and has three locks.

Going up! *Hebe* ascending the first lock.

MONDAY 13TH AUGUST

That morning we had several wet spells. The Gunner put it down to our sailing on a Friday. We managed to set sail, however, and although there was a strong headwind, and several showers, we managed to make fairly good progress.

About 10 a.m. we were about to pass a house at the side of which were a number of stables for boat horses. The Gunner declared that he knew the occupier and that whenever they passed that way he called in. Taking the water can he landed and knocked. He was soon answered and obtained the water. It then occurred to him that we were in need of eggs, so he inquired of the lady and was supplied with some. But then it was necessary to pay for the eggs and he had only a ten shilling note, she had not change. Then a remarkable thing happened. In spite of the Gunner's physiognomy the lady told him to pay some other time. She was very trusting. We passed that house perhaps once a year on average. The matter was satisfactorily settled a little later. Soon after the Gunner had caught up with the *Hebe* we passed the lady's husband and, as the Commander had change, we there and then paid for the eggs.

A little later we passed Church Minshull, a delightful old world village. Leaving the Stewardess and the Gunner in the boat the other two set off to buy some provisions. From the canal all one sees of the hamlet is a winding lane disappearing among a clump of trees.

Proceeding along this country lane one passes over the River Weaver which here is only a good-sized stream, whereas a little further down it bears great boats on its bosom and is a commercial highway.

Church Minshull.

The first sign of life in Church Minshull is a black and white cottage with an enormously thick thatch. This on further inspection is found to be not the birthplace of Henry Shakespeare, nor yet of William Ford. Neither Queen Elizabeth[3] nor Cromwell seem to have slept there. Far from it – this charming cottage is the headquarters of two banks and a hen run.

Disappointed in this the two travellers found recompense further on. The Parish Church looked very fine, but then like Jerome K. Jerome (whose memory may remain forever green) we do not belong to that class of people who, on arriving at a strange town, immediately rush off to the church to inspect the graves of former inhabitants. No. What delighted the Commander and the Powder Monkey was the sign of the village inn.

It represented an old badger and must have been painted by a master. There stood Brock, on the greenest of swards, four sturdy legs upholding his longish body with his snout gleaming whitely. It was indeed worth the glass which protected it from the weather.

As for the rest of the village it consisted of a row of cottages and a shop. The shop was typical of all villages like this one and held everything. On account of continually remembering things that we needed no less than four separate journeys had to be made to this shop.

The day continuing to be rather wet, we only succeeded in making a lot of little trips during the fine intervals. Accordingly we did not make much progress and stopped at Barbridge Junction, the *Hebe* being hove-to near a big reservoir. Just as it was getting dark a great flapping noise was heard. Then there was a commotion from the Commander who was shouting to the Gunner to come and look. The latter, in some alarm and thinking the reservoir must have burst, poked his head out from the boat and was astonished to see a great flock of wild geese winging their way overhead and calling to each other as they settled on the surface of the reservoir for the night.

Following their example we too were soon settled down and asleep.

---

3. This is, of course, Elizabeth I. The future Elizabeth II had been born on 21 April 1926 and was thus only 2½ at the time.

Chapter IV

Traffic – The Welsh Canal –
Swing Bridges – Grindley Brook –
First wind in our favour – Bettisfield

TUESDAY 14TH AUGUST

'A fresh breeze and cloudless sky' is to be found on consulting the Gunner's log, a marked contrast to the day before. The weather being favourable the Commander, to whom a dirty boat is anathema, seized the opportunity to give the *Hebe* a good sluicing. It's amazing the way dirt collects in a boat. You take it out in a spotless condition and in half an hour it is cluttered with muddy footmarks, bits of grass, lumps of newspaper, strings, and a host of bric-a-brac.

The Commander said he couldn't understand it. He said if you took a clean boat and deposited it in the middle of the Atlantic Ocean, sailed away and then returned in two hours, the boat would probably be loaded up with all sorts of rubbish. Therefore, as the *Hebe* had not been washed for about four days, she needed it now very badly.

The operations were regarded with great delectation by the crews of a number of barges which went by. That number even including several motor barges.

This canal[1] is one of the busiest. It is a good route between the ports of the Mersey and the Dee and the Midlands. Now here's one in the eye for those who say canals are absolutely dead – there is life in the old bird yet. Between nine and eleven o'clock four lots of motor barges passed, each lot carrying from 40 to 60 tons[2] of materials, and about a dozen ordinary monkey boats

---

1. The Shropshire Union main line.
2. 40 to 60 tons if the motor boats had butties in tow; otherwise this is something of an overestimate.

The Commander at work.

went by, each with from 20 to 30 tons. At a conservative estimate this means in all about four hundred tons. Think of the number of lorries required to carry this amount.

At about eleven o'clock as the sky clouded over we thought it wise to pack up and had to set off against a strong headwind. After about two miles we turned the corner and entered the Welsh Branch of the Shropshire Union and there were immediately three locks to ascend.

This cheered the heart of the Gunner who was rather morose as a result of the continuous headwind. *En passant* it may be remarked that his idea of Paradise seems to be a succession of locks up and down which one can travel all day, everlastingly meeting and passing the time o'day with millions of barge folk.

The next place of stoppage was a small village known by the romantic-sounding name of Ravensmoor. Here we laid in another store of provisions, and a short way past Ravensmoor a halt was made while the Commander performed miracles of cooking with a gargantuan rasher of ham wreathed in tomatoes.

While dining in the lee of a bridge the *Arcturus* glided by.

There is no word in the whole of the English language which so completely and satisfyingly expresses the motion of a canal boat as 'glide'. First the patient horse, with the peculiar walk of these animals, goes by with a big belt of gaily coloured beads[3] rubbing his side. Trailing out behind him is the bouncing, whistling, towrope. Then some minutes later the prow of the barge approaches. The boat creeps by without a sound. Foot by foot, yard by yard. No haste. No frantic buffeting of the water. No tumultuous wake. It is like a ghost. No sound except perhaps the sigh of the rushes or the creek of the rudder. In these days of the motor car one can derive great pleasure and tranquility from the movement of a boat like this.

Stevenson knew about this. Here is what he says about a barge:

> Of all the creatures of commercial enterprise the canal barge is by far the most delightful to consider. It may spread its sails, and then you see it sailing high above the tree tops and the windmill, sailing on the aqueduct; sailing though green cornlands, the most picturesque of things amphibious. Or the horse plods along at a foot pace as if there were no such thing as business in the world; and the man dreaming at the tiller sees the same spire on the horizon all day long.
>
> It is a mystery how things ever get to their destination at this rate; and to see the barges waiting their turn at a lock affords a fine lesson of how easily the world may be taken.

---

3. Actually called bobbins.

There should be many contented spirits on board, for such a life is both to travel and to stay at home.

The chimney smokes for dinner as you go along; the banks of the canal slowly unroll their scenery to contemplative eyes; the barge floats by great forests and through great cities with their public buildings and their lamps at night; and for the bargee, in his floating home, 'travelling abed', it is merely as if he were listening to another man's story or turning the leaves of a book in which he had no concern. He may take his afternoon walk in some foreign country on the banks of the canal, and come home to dinner at his own fireside.

After dinner we passed on through some fine bits of canal scenery. The banks had lately been tended and their soft greenness was reflected in the placid surface of the wide canal with beautiful effect. Overhead, through the lacery of great overhanging trees, the sun shone from a bright blue sky flecked with cumuli and revealed everything to the eye with that pleasant light which comes after rain in summer.

Wrenbury is a charmingly old village complete with a green surrounded by black and white low thatched cottages. While returning from a tour of inspection the Stewardess and the Powder Monkey lighted on a great patch of mushrooms, which formed a welcome addition to breakfast next morning.

It was just past Wrenbury that we met a new type of swingbridge – or rather a drawbridge. Instead of being pushed round like those in home waters, they went up and down like the old fashioned bridges at castle gates. Usually swingbridges are by way of a curiosity on the canal. Long before you reach them you are speculating whether or not someone is going to open it for you. The usual crowd of natives is of course paralysed by the sight of the boat and cannot lend a hand. All they can do is wonder how your mast will pass the bridge. Generally they decide that you will either 'take it down' or 'have to carry it round'. When, however, one disembarks and proceeds to swing the bridge – even though the bridge be nigh immovable – they are so moonstruck that no one will lend a hand, but all stand like so many skittles waiting to be pushed over. To do them justice, however, it must be said that in the South and on such rivers as the Severn and Avon rustics are in general far more obliging than in the North.

In the early evening we overtook our friends in the *Arcturus*. As we were in strange waters we inquired of them as to accommodation further on. 'The Duck' at Quoisley seemed to be a favourite with the mate, but the captain said that the Grindley Brook Arms had more superior facilities.

Therefore we put our backs into it and about 8.30 after ascending a short flight of nine locks we entered Grindley Brook where, as usual, the Stewardess and the Powder Monkey slept, leaving the other two in charge of

Wrenbury church.

the boat. Shortly after supper we had an instance of the way in which canal boats are able to go a long way in a relatively short time. The *Arcturus* came up on the locks, and after giving the horse half an hour on his nosebag harnessed up and resumed their way. In answer to the Gunner's shouted question they informed us that on long lockless stretches they marched all night. This is how it is done. They may not go fast, but as they keep on going they make good time.

WEDNESDAY 15TH AUGUST

The Stewardess and the Powder Monkey rather delayed things by arriving an hour late for breakfast. They came up to find the hardy ones gnashing their teeth on account of losing the breeze which a turn in the canal had brought into our favour. It transpired later that they had not been called because the landlord, or lady, had some niece or nephew who was about to be or had just been married. In spite of these conjugal facilities we cast off and hoisted sail at about 11 a.m.

Thus we continued for many miles, although not perhaps at a striking pace. The wind was with us until soon after tea when we had to turn at right-angles to our course. This brought the wind ahead and we had to use our muscles and row.

For some miles the canal ran through a great stretch of bog land, a most remarkable change of scenery.

Although we had intended to put up at Ellesmere for the night we eventually had to stop at Bettisfield, some distance short of Ellesmere.

The Stewardess and Powder Monkey found lodging at 'The Nag's Head', a pretty hostelry kept by a charming old couple. The Commander and the Gunner, however, were not so fortunate. The canal was very much silted up and they had to spend over half an hour pulling the *Hebe* up and down making numerous soundings. At last they found a berth and soon turned in.

Chapter V

The world is a small place – Ellesmere –
Luxury Boats – The Tunnel at Chirk –
Arcturus again – Our first Welshman

THURSDAY 16TH AUGUST

On consulting the Gunner's log we find 'Late start on account of the idlers. Stiff headwind and dull sky'. Soon afterwards, however, we came to a favourable turn and did a little sailing. This occupation failing to propel us forwards we put the Gunner ashore with the end of the towrope in his hand.

About two miles from Ellesmere as we were approaching a short tunnel we noticed, standing on the bank and regarding us with great interest, a man. As the boat neared him the Commander let out a yell to stop to the Gunner and hastily steered the boat in. He bounded out and fell upon this man's neck and wept (metaphorically speaking). It thereafter transpired that the individual and the Commander had in the past worked side by side for many years. They had not seen each other for about 20 years, so that it was most remarkable that they should meet here.

Passing through the tunnel and then by a long plantation of walnut trees, we came near Ellesmere, and for a mile or so ran along the side of a beautiful mere. We entered the town by rowing up a long dock[1] and moored the *Hebe* under a big milk depot. The usual three disembarked and went into the town, the Commander being left in charge of the *Hebe*. As has before been remarked, the Commander in his affable manner has a little way with him. It so happened that while looking after the *Hebe* – that is while lying back

---

1. The 'Ellesmere Branch' is a spur about a quarter of a mile long.

Ellesmere Tunnel, from a contemporary postcard.

Ellesmere Junction, from a contemporary postcard.

The mere from gardens at Ellesmere, from a contemporary postcard.

and smoking his pipe – he got into conversation with the owner of the milk depot. This man was so delighted at meeting one who was so obviously a circumnavigator of the globe that he wanted to load us with presents as is done in the East. In this case, however, with a slight modification. What really happened was that the owner insisted on filling numerous receptacles with milk for us.

Ellesmere itself is not a very interesting or a very imposing town. It is an odd mixture of ancient and modern, of cobblestones and Macadam, but beyond this there is not much either to see or to admire.

As we were passing out of Ellsemere we went by a wharf where was moored a luxury motor barge, a thing of cabins and curtains all picked out in black and white. The Stewardess and the Powder Monkey were loud in their praises of this boat. Not so the Commander and the Gunner.

'Huh! Wouldn't touch it with a lump of soap on a forty-foot barge pole!'

The Commander and the Gunner have a rooted objection to motorboats and to luxury boats on the canal. Given only the ghost of a chance and they will both launch into yards and yards of rhetoric about 'wanting a tall ship with some heavenly body wherewith to navigate it'. It is only a detail, but

Above: The aqueduct and viaduct at Chirk.

Right: Contemporary postcard of the Chirk aqueduct.

The Powder
Monkey
surveys Chirk.

beyond knowing how to haul on a rope and being able to spot the Pole Star neither knows the least thing about the art of navigation.

Round about 5 o'clock to our great surprise we came upon two locks. It had been thought that the last lock on the outward voyage was at Grindley Brook, but lo! Here were two locks[2] which had evidently sprung up in the night. They were certainly not on the map.

Approaching Chirk we were astonished to find the air grow suddenly warmer. So far it had been rather chilly that day, but as if relenting the air grew really balmy. The canal, which for many miles had been winding in and out in the Vale of Llangollen, now turned and by means of an enormous aqueduct[3] now crossed the Vale. At the end of the aqueduct is the famous tunnel which was, when constructed, thought to be a veritable marvel. It is over a quarter of a mile in length[4] but is not very wide. Two barges can just pass in it. The roof is low and the towing path (although guarded by a rail) is not too safe on account of the numerous hummocks and potholes.

We went through the tunnel in this way: the Gunner went ahead in order to clear the way or to give warning. The Commander took the rope and towed while the Powder Monkey endeavoured to steer by the light of occasional matches struck by the Stewardess.

All would have been well had it not been for the Powder Monkey who tried to steer not by regarding the tiny star of light at the far end but by taking bearings from the invisible sides. The natural result was that the

---

2. Most likely New Martin Bottom and Top locks, just after Frankton Junction.
3. Chirk Aqueduct, uniquely, has a railway viaduct above and alongside it.
4. 459 yards, with a towpath running through.

aforesaid invisible sides of the tunnel kept continually coming out of the dark and hitting the boat, to the great detriment of the Commander's beautiful varnish.

This stone tunnel was succeeded by another tunnel of wood. The light did come through the trees in places but it was dark as a forest and very quiet.

When eventually we did come out into the open it was to find ourselves near a stone loading wharf at which our old friend, *Arcturus*, was moored. We learned from them that Vron was distant only a few miles and boasted some good hotels.

Putting the best foot forward we soon came to Vron. At first there was some difficulty in finding beds as the whole village seemed to have gone to the Shrewsbury flower show. All ended happily, and we turned in after a lengthy conversation held across the canal with a genuine Welshman.

Chapter VI

*The great superiority of boating over any other form
of pleasure – The Flyboat – Vale of Llangollen –
Reminiscences of the Commander – The wind with us
– Chirk tunnel again – Bettisfield*

FRIDAY 17TH AUGUST

The morning broke fine and sunny with every promise of the day being hot.
Having breakfasted we made what was for us an early start. We soon came
to another aqueduct, very like the one at Chirk, but this time there was no
tunnel at the end.[1]

The canal here is altogether delightful. It runs in a meandering sort of way in
and out among the trees, half way up the slope of the Vale of Llangollen. At times
the canal came alongside the road to the town which was fairly busy with trippers
in motors going to Llangollen. We had therefore plenty of opportunities of
basking in the envious gaze of these inferior animals – the devotees of the petrol
engine – who were no doubt created for the sole purpose of showing in high
relief the numerous advantages enjoyed by those who take their pleasure afloat.

As we were proceeding at a gentle pace in this serene frame of mind, we
were suddenly dumbfounded by the advent of a crowded flyboat,[2] a thing we
thought belonged solely to an earlier age.

---

1. Considering the stature and importance of the great Pontcysyllte Aqueduct, ADS gives
   remarkably little attention to it!
2. On a similar trip, much later in the 1960s, the flyboats were still running. I remember
   the 'navigable feeder' section after the aqueduct (4 or 5 miles) was much improved with
   concrete walls to the channel, even though it was only a little more than one boat wide
   in places. The water is collected at the Horseshoe Falls, about a mile past Llangollen, and
   feeds down to Trevor and thence via the canal to the SU main line.

Hebe crosses the Pontcysyllte Aqueduct.

The view from the Pontcysyllte Aqueduct.

The Pontcysyllte Aqueduct, from a contemporary postcard.

The canal was narrow here, and as we went on it became narrower. A remarkable phenomenon was observed by the Gunner who was greatly puzzled for some time. Usually the water in a canal is near-stagnant but this canal was actually flowing. The weeds hanging from the bottom all streamed out in the same direction so there was obviously a strong current. We were all mystified until it dawned on us that this canal was really the tap which kept the other canals full of water.

At about 11.30 we reached our destination, that town of old ladies – Llangollen. It was filled with sticky trippers and dusty tourists from Rochdale and Heckmondwike, all with weird headgear and sucking rock. Except for that feature Llangollen is very pretty; the view on each side of the bridge is especially beautiful.

We did not stay long in Llangollen. After collecting letters and admiring the view from the bridge and taking dinner we turned the *Hebe*'s bow homewards.

Just passing a gap in the trees which lined the lower side we caught a glimpse of the River Dee. When the Commander saw it he smiled and informed us that this was the spot from which he had launched a boat many years ago. It

Right: The view from Langollen bridge.

Below: The village of Langollen, from a contemporary postcard.

Above and left: Two contemporary postcards of the 'flyboat' at Llangollen; on a later trip in the 1960s, they were certainly horse-drawn.

seemed that he and a friend had set out from Chester by canal and reached Llangollen. Here, instead of returning by canal, they carried the boat below the falls and launched it on the Dee. The return voyage by river went very smoothly until they reached the aqueduct at Chirk. Here, in shooting the rapids, they had the misfortune to stove-in the boat. After hauling their vessel ashore and unloading the baggage (by which time a crowd had collected) they inspected the damage. This was such that they offered the boat and sold it for thirty shillings.

The sun was shining strongly and the wind, although in our favour, was so desultory that it would not have flickered a candle flame. Therefore we decided to take what the gods offered – by way of a flowing canal – and let the stream drift us.

It was just as well we had not been too energetic because after a little while we discovered we had left behind the camera. Mooring the boat, the Powder Monkey and the Gunner returned to Llangollen and were fortunate enough to find it.

Having started again we soon came out of the shelter of a tall cliff and found a light breeze. So, hoisting the Jolly Roger, we commenced that long, long sail which was to take us right home without the necessity of touching oar or towrope.

As we approached the tunnel at Chirk the Gunner, remembering the amount of varnish left on the walls before, gave the Commander a long towrope, and giving vent to several imitation nautical terms took the yoke-lines and steered the boat through without mishap. This having been safely accomplished and the aqueduct having been passed we came to rest at a little village near Chirk.

SATURDAY 18TH AUGUST

In the early morning while the Commander and Gunner were busy putting things shipshape they were visited by a crowd of swans and cygnets. After a little persuasion these became so tame as to eat out of the Gunner's hand.

The day was again bright and hot. In fact the Powder Monkey and the Gunner, who went into Chirk for films and provisions, found that in spite of the scenery the three-mile walk was too hot altogether.

On the return of the forage party we found the breeze still favourable, and so hoisting sail we glided away and were able to have dinner below New Martin lock.

All afternoon was spent in the same way. Pleasantly drifting along through the quiet countryside with sails spread. After tea, however, we hurried in

Cygnet ring.

The view astern.
A horse-drawn
narrowboat is
just visible in the
distance.

order to reach Ellesmere before the shops shut. The next day was Sunday, so
we had to get there before closing time or go hungry on the Sabbath.

There was plenty of time when we got there and after stocking up we
again set out and were fortunate enough to reach Bettisfield for the night.
The Stewardess and Powder Monkey again slept at 'The Nag's Head' but, as
before, the *Hebe* was not so fortunate. The Commander and Gunner had to
go on about a mile to find a good anchorage by a great cornfield in which
the stooks were standing.

Chapter VII

Sunday – The Gunner's recreation –
Fishing competitions – Grindley Brook

SUNDAY 19TH AUGUST

The spell of fine weather was still holding, and when the Commander and Gunner awoke the countryside was bathed in sunshine while a hidden bellringer gently worked his art in some distant tower. There was that indefinable something in the atmosphere by which one knows without the aid of calendars or almanacs what day of the week it is. There is a stillness or something akin to a feel in the air which, even if there is a half-gale blowing or the rain is pouring down, makes one as certain as if it had been bawled in one's ear that it is Sunday. Through this silence – if you so like to call it – there comes the noise of the woodpecker or the note of the cuckoo, even though the bird is miles away. A grasshopper whirrs and the sound strikes the ear like a dozen threshing machines. But when the immediate noise ends there is that silence again, which is yet not silence. Nature is always murmuring secrets but her conversation is unlike that of humans. It fits into the general scheme of things exactly as an oak tree or a water hen. It is only human noises which – 'Oh, I beg your pardon, really I quite forgot.'

The Stewardess and the Powder Monkey, oblivious to all the aforementioned charms, arrived in time for breakfast. At least they would have arrived if breakfast had been postponed by two hours.

And after breakfasting there stole upon our ears, especially the Gunner's, the sound of the local carillon. Upon which we packed up our goods and chattels and rowed back towards Bettisfield where, leaving the Gunner in charge, the other three walked down the lane to church. The Gunner was not put out at this seeming neglect and on the contrary thoroughly enjoyed the time spent alone in charge of the *Hebe*. When the others had disappeared he proceeded to clear away the most conspicuous of the Commander's pipes, various books belonging to the Powder Monkey and after that a huge collection of odds and ends such as bights of rope, grease pot covers, hay, dead flowers, old coats and any mortal thing.

Next the Gunner turned attention to the gear. The oars were laid nicely in their proper positions and the cushions were placed so as to catch the eye. Then a masterstroke. He took the painter, the towrope, the halyard and the sheet and coiled each one into great round target-like mats, a wonder to behold. Indeed, on the others' return they were almost overcome.

After dinner we lazily drifted on. The favouring breeze had died to the merest zephyr except for a few stronger puffs, rare and far between. Towards four o'clock we hit upon a fishing competition and many were the remarks heralding our passing. As we went by, the words exchanged between two yokels were delightful:

1st Yokel: 'Could'st mannypilate a sail like yon George?'

George: 'Naw!'

1st Yokel (mournfully reminiscent): 'Eh! I once got in an awful mess wi' a contraption like that at Morecambe Bay.'

Unfortunately we then passed out of earshot but the yokel's tone was really suggestive.

Having reached the end of the competition we unpacked the box and had tea, after which we gently sailed on to Grindley Brook.[1]

As we passed the turning point to Whitchurch, which place we had visited, we were astounded to find that the natives had actually lifted the bridge at our approach. Accommodation at Grindley Brook was found at the same hotel as on the outward voyage.

---

1. Of the six locks at Grindley Brook, the upper three – locks 17, 18 and 19 – are in fact a triple staircase, something which ADS, again, seems to have ignored.

Chapter VIII

Crowding on sail – The lock keeper's son –
Wrenbury – Accident in a squall – Good mileage –
Progress in the wet – Calveley – Becoming bargees

MONDAY 20TH AUGUST

'Nine o'clock and a wet morning, wind strong and favourable' is the statement found in the Gunner's log. We swept away at a round pace about 11.30. The wind was all that could be desired, and so after descending the six locks at Grindley Brook we hoisted the mainsail and tore away at a spanking pace. At first, thinking the wind too strong, we refrained from setting the mizzen.

'Pooh!' said the Gunner, 'set more sail in many a stiffer breeze. This is only a puff, quite safe if you stand by to let go.'

Accordingly the mizzen was set, and with the crew perched on the weather gunwhale we swept along at a good nine or ten knots.

A little later our course was impeded by two locks. The lock keeper (besides keeping locks) also kept hens and was able to supply us with eggs. The Commander, anxious not to lose any wind, was perhaps over-hasty in the way he packed the eggs, for on coming to open the tin the next day we found three smashed.

The lock keeper's wee son came out and stared at the *Hebe* so interestedly and in such a comical manner that the Stewardess offered him a ride. This was rather a different thing than just looking on and he began to draw back, but his mother, coming out at that moment, accepted the ride for him. It was bad enough for him just sitting in the boat, but when the sail was set and the *Hebe* began to heel over his heart reached his mouth. He gave one despairing look astern and cowered down in the bottom of this crank concern worked

Above and below: Two pictures of Wrenbury (probably commercial prints).

WRENBURY GREEN

by madmen and prepared to meet his destruction. The look of relief on his face as he scuttled home when we put him ashore would have moved the heart of a criminal.

Dinner over, we continued our glorious sail until about four o'clock as we were approaching Wrenbury. We were bounding along at a good rate with the breeze increasing bit by bit. Then it happened. A squall far more violent than we had yet experienced struck the *Hebe* with all its force. The boat did her best but could not obey the wind readily enough, and with a crack the step of the mast was wrenched out.

Luckily Wrenbury was nearby. Leaving the Gunner in charge, the others went off to find material for repairing the damage. This was soon accomplished and then, it being about five o'clock, we brewed a dish of tea.

Originally we had intended to stop at Wrenbury for the night but the wind had stood us so well, and was still blowing, that we decided to make for Nantwich. However, we did not reach Nantwich, for at the end of this branch of the canal we found excellent accommodation near Barbridge. So as the sky was not looking too well we stopped there for the night.

TUESDAY 21ST AUGUST

The sky's promise of the night before was fulfilled, and so we were held up by the rain. Now the Gunner has studied the art of towing and this stood us in good stead. He suggested towing with a rope to each end of the boat. By this means the person towing would be able to steer the boat, and therefore if the horse could steer, the boat would be able to progress and still keep the covers up. His advice was followed, with the result that we were soon in Nantwich.

Most of the morning was spent in purchasing provisions and looking round the town, which is a quaint old place. By the time the forage party had returned the weather had lifted and we were able to roll up the covers and set off.

About a mile or so from Nantwich we discovered a grassy bank in the lee of a pine wood. It looked so inviting, and was so obviously made for a meal, that no sooner had we seen it than we pulled in, and were soon wrapping ourselves round an excellent dinner. That finished, we drifted onwards to reach Barbridge, and instead of turning we continued straight on towards Calveley. This was not reached but we had tea some miles short of it.

After tea we held a council of war and decided that, as there was a day or two in hand thanks to the wind, we would return to the house of kettle

The Square, Nantwich.

Left and below: Two views of Nantwich, from contemporary postcards.

where we had stopped the night before. Accordingly we hoisted sail and the wind, serving well, blew us along quite nicely.

Nearing Barbridge some people showed great interest in the sail. This, naturally, caused the wind to die down. It is a remarkable thing how a wind, which having blown a boat for miles and miles, will die as soon as one approaches a crowd of onlookers and has a chance to show off. It is either magic or auto-suggestion. No sooner does a crowd appear than the wind fades away.

It is much the same with a novice in the boat. For miles the novice will steer a boat like any old shell back, but as soon as a crowd appears every rope is the wrong one, and in the confusion the boat gets run aground.

After reaching port we still had plenty of time and so hung about for a while. Very soon along came a barge with another empty barge in tow. They were bound for Oswestry and so had to ascend the locks. This we regarded as an opportunity for doing our daily good turn. While the full barge was being worked up by the professionals we, the amateurs, proceeded to work up the butty boat. What an exciting time, manhandling the long heavy thing between the locks, steering it from the little platform, while the real crew looked on with smiles of amusement. Nevertheless they were full of thanks when we delivered their charge safe and sound.

When questioned by the Gunner they declared that they had, that day, travelled with one horse towing two barges and twenty-five tons of goods from Ellesmere Port – forty-two miles away.

Chapter IX

*Calveley – The Irish Mail – Strange encounter with
a barge – Church Minshull – The wind again –
Middlewich – Remarkable canal water*

WEDNESDAY 22ND AUGUST

The morning being fine we seized the opportunity to clean the *Hebe* and
thus made a late start. Having started we made for Calveley where provisions
were obtained, and while waiting there, where the canal is in close proximity
to the railway, we saw the *Irish Mail* thunder by. Accordingly when we started
again we were privileged to hear a long harangue from various members of
the crew on the joys of boating.

Just after dining on a grassy bank on the Wardle Branch, the rain began to
patter and we hastily packed the remains and rigged the cover. The weather
did not show any sign of clearing up, so remembering our previous feats with
the towing line we attached two ropes and went gaily along down locks and
through pounds.

While the Commander was taking a spell at the tow rope there occurred
the Great Adventure. To those under the cover the fact that a barge was
approaching was quite unknown until the horse drew level with the boat.
The animal was then stopped with the intention of letting the *Hebe* float
over the submerged towline.[1] We had nearly crossed it when, suddenly, the
horse took fright and started to move, thus tightening the towline. The result
was that the line was caught in our rudder, and with startling suddenness the
Hebe began to move backwards. About three bargees shoved, the Commander

---

1. Towlines were, more often than not, of cotton rope which sank when wet, rather than the
   heavier hemp or sisal. Floating over a line in such a way was not uncommon.

shouted, the Gunner shouted, dogs barked and kittens mewed. The horse stopped and the rope was freed. Had the horse started sooner, or had it not stopped at all, there would indeed have been a catastrophe. Luckily nothing serious happened and we continued on our way unharmed.

The rain was still pouring down when we arrived at Church Minshull where, as we had promised ourselves on the outward journey, we stopped for the night at the 'Old Badger'.

THURSDAY 23RD AUGUST

Yesterday's foul weather had been blown clear by the same old wind which had brought us so far on the homeward voyage, and which was blowing freshly. The Jolly Roger was spread and we flew away at a fine pace, so that we actually overtook a smart barge which had passed us nearly an hour before we started.

Middlewich was reached in time for dinner, which meal was taken after buying some provisions and rowing back to a more or less secluded spot. After that we descended the last lock on this branch[2] and went up King's Lock on the Trent and Mersey Canal. A remarkable phenomenon was experienced in this lock. Brunner Mond's works lay in close proximity to the canal at this point, and they evidently threw waste matter into the canal because the water was a beautiful green tint. When the *Hebe* was in the lock with the water cascading in a huge froth came on the surface. This froth gradually reached the level of the gunwhale, and rising further still began to topple in.
It was necessary to do something at once, so the Commander took an oar and managed to keep the level down by scooping great bladesful off the top. It was exciting while it lasted but soon the gate was opened and the *Hebe* slid into the open.

After this incident, owing to a turn in the canal, we found the wind was no longer serving us, and for the first time on the homeward trip had seriously to turn to the oars. After ascending the next two locks there were clamourings for tea, especially from the Gunner who said that having worked the boat through so many locks in the broiling sun he at least deserved some sustenance. Tea was augmented by an itinerant ice-cream merchant which helped us enjoy the sun, and afterwards we pushed on in the beautiful evening, reaching Wheelock where good beds for the night were found.

---

2. Stanthorne Lock, No. 3.

Chapter X

Locks, locks, locks – Need of provisions – Puzzle
of classification – Deluge – Sunset at Kent Green –
Stowaway – Waterflowers – Macclesfield

FRIDAY 24TH AUGUST

We made an early start because from Wheelock to Harecastle the canal consists of one lock after another. The sun was shining fiercely and on account of this we took things easily, slowly gaining the top of this water staircase.

At Rock Heath we found it necessary to buy provisions. Indeed, whether it was due to the fresh air or not, while on the canal we had to stock up at nearly every town or village we went through. It was usually like this: On nearing a town somebody would say: 'Now, here are some shops. Surely we are in need of something?' Another would answer: 'Well, there's only a dozen eggs and two loaves with a pound and a half of bacon. We'd better get something to be on the safe side.' And so the capacity of the boat already loaded to Plimsoll's eye would be further strained.

Everywhere we go crowds gather with staring eyes and gaping mouths. The remarks passed by these gatherings are truly amusing and often incredible in a maritime nation like ours. The *Hebe* is placed in classes of ships and boats which the builders have never heard of. We will be gently gliding along admiring the scenery when suddenly a scream will rend the air, followed by some such remark as: 'Oh! A yacht coming. Come and look at the yacht Mary Jane.'

At other times we are termed only a cock-boat. But are we cast down? A thousand times no. In about ten minutes we are metamorphosed into a ship and have in all seriousness been classed as a motor boat. Frequently we are welcomed by the cry: 'Oxford and Cambridge!' Not, mark you, merely

Oxford or just Cambridge, but we become either two racing eights or else a representative crew of both these universities – quite a compliment. However, we attained our crowning success near Church Lawton where our approach was heralded by: 'Eh! Come and look. A submarine!'

We reached the top of the flight safely and had tea just before Hall Green. We were sitting down near a big bridge after eating when a storm came. Hastily packing, we ran into the shelter of the bridge while the rain poured down in torrents. The thunder thundered and the lightning lightninged for about an hour.

Then with great rapidity the weather cleared, and with everything steaming and freshly scented we pushed on as far as Kent Green where we stopped for the night. The sky, in order to make up for the wet, treated us to a glorious sunset. The heavens were so red that the Gunner, under the boat cover, thought a haystack must be on fire and accordingly pushed out his head to see it.

Thistle, a butty working for the Anderton Company Ltd.

Homeward bound.

SATURDAY 25TH AUGUST

The Commander awoke in the morning and rubbed his eyes in astonishment. He blinked, but still the vision persisted. There, lying on his pillow, was a small kitten. It had crept on board in the wet during the night and had contentedly gone to sleep. When woken up it stumbled about in an uncertain way and was found later to be blind, we were told, due to the depredations of rats.

The wind was blowing nicely, and so hoisting the sail we were soon spanking along over some beautiful scenery. The water, owing to a scarcity of boats, was very clear, and for the same reason marvellous forests grow on the floor of the canal. Great green trees, cabbages and flowers flourish. Shoals of fish wind in and out. In fact the underwater scenery equals any description of submarine coral caves in the tropics. The over-water scenery also flourished. Lillies grew so thick that at times the *Hebe* was seriously impeded.

Last lock.

But these things, like good companions, stupid people early cease to observe: and the Abstract Bagman tittups past in his spring gig, and is positively not aware of the flowers along the lane, or the scenery of the weather overhead.

(Stephenson)

We soon reached Bosley locks, having dinner between the fifth and sixth. A slight shower held us up for a while but it was not much. After the last lock we spread every inch of canvas and gently neared Macclesfield, reaching the town about eight o'clock. We foolishly passed on again after stocking up, with the result that darkness found us still moving. After vainly inquiring for rooms we at last stumbled across a farmhouse where lodging for the night was obtained.

Chapter XI

Last Day

SUNDAY 26TH AUGUST

Of our last day there is not a great deal to recount. There are no notes in the Gunner's log and what information we have is gleaned from memories of the crew.

The wind was still holding and took us along quite well during the morning. From Macclesfield on to Bollington there stretched a fishing competition of over three hundred more-or-less experts.

Dinner and tea were both taken near port. At these meals we endeavoured to consume as much food as possible in order to save carrying it home.

The sun was shining very strongly so we did not make very good progress. Indeed, we only caught the eight o'clock train by the skin of our teeth. Right at the very end, as if sorry to lose us the sky wept copiously. This of course only made us travel quicker and enabled us to reach home in time for supper.

That's all.[1]

---

1. As far as I can judge, this first trip covered approximately 192 miles and 136 locks in total.

HISTORICAL MISCELLANY
1929

30 March	Imperial Airways begins flights from London to Karachi.
31 May	A Hung Parliament results after the General Election – Liberals hold the balance of power.
7 June	Conservatives concede.
8 June	Ramsay Macdonald forms a Labour Government.
24 October	BBC begins experimental TV transmissions. Wall Street Crashes.
2 December	The first telephone boxes are established in London.

ALSO:

Leon Trotsky is expelled from the Soviet Union.

Herbert Hoover is President of the USA.

The first Academy Awards (Oscars) ceremony is held.

From a weather point of view it was one of the severest winters of the twentieth century (up to 1939/40). During the January and February months in Hampshire, 150 hours of continuous frost was reported and ice floes were reported in the lower Thames & Estuary. Notable were very heavy snow storms. From January to April a drought affected Britain with only about 50 per cent of normal rainfall. But by November there was exceptionally heavy daily rainfall.

BOOK TWO

HEBE IN THE COUNTRY
1929

With a Foreword by The Owner

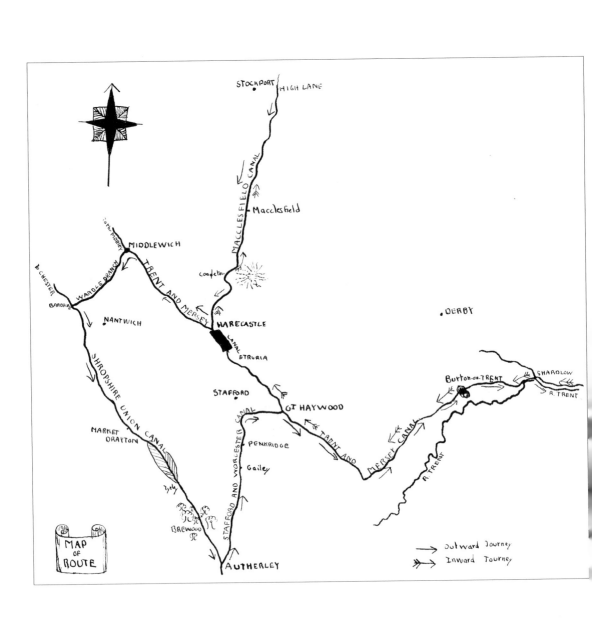

Foreword

To readers who have not perused previous records of the doings of the *Hebe*
I would advise them that this journal refers to the wanderings on Inland
Waters of a two pair, inrigged boat, which, whilst it may usually be found
on the placid waters of the Macclesfield Canal, each year ventures forth on a
more hazardous journey, visiting Rivers and Canals as far as possible strange
to both boat and crew.

The crew usually consists of the Owner and his family, or possibly someone
or other of the family being absent, a friend may also be one of the family.

In the course of many years of travel a number of waterways have become
familiar, but it is always a pleasure to revisit old scenes and there are still many
places yet to be visited, which lends a stimulus to greater effort to reach
them.

To one content to travel at a comparatively slow pace and who can find
pleasure in the rustic scene, watching the ways of bird and fish life, the quiet
but persistent lap of water on a boat, a trip on the narrow waters of a canal or
on the broad bosom of such a river as the Trent may give a new zest to life.

Such a holiday is all-sufficient for the Owner and seems to be equally so
for the 'crew', judging by the frequent references made to it during the rest
of the year.

Various duties such as cooking, looking after the stores or the boat are
allotted to individual members of the crew, and to one who has a literary turn
is entrusted 'the Keeping of the Log'. For the future pleasure of all who care
to read an account of the trip, this task we will now leave to him.

The Owner

Hebe at home.

Chapter I

High Lane to Autherley

SATURDAY 10TH AUGUST

At long last, 'Cast her off' from the Commander, and the *Hebe* gently glided into the waters of the Macclesfield Canal.

We were bound for Nottingham with a cargo of foodstuffs. At least, we were certainly bound for Nottingham, and we were loaded for the most part with eatables, a statement which is not to be interpreted as meaning that we had a cargo of edibles *for* Nottingham. Far from it. These comestibles were only by way of providing the necessary sustenance for the crew for one or two days.

The Crew on this occasion amounted to a grand total of two. The Commander and the Mate. The absence of others who usually form a crew did not deter us in the least. Did not the Mate proudly possess a sextant (left behind) and a pocket knife with scores of instruments? And had not the Commander a large collection of pipes on board? Thus equipped we pushed on with dauntless hearts.

The sun was bright and warm. Hardly a breath of wind stirred the limpid waters of the canal as we rowed along the borders of two counties. At Bollington the mill was unusually quiet. There was a strike on and the machinery was idle. White Nancy still defied the elements from the top of her hill and was sharply defined against the sky in her new white coat, proudly indicating the highest point in Cheshire.

A halt was called for tea at a little place just outside Macclesfield in a spinney of gnarled Hawthorne trees. While tea was in progress three aeroplanes flew about overhead performing various tricks, no doubt for our especial benefit. Tea over, we gently paddled on under an absolutely cloudless sky. The fact that Macclesfield Carnival was in progress did not deter many people from

Bosley Cloud.

either fishing or staring over walls as we went by, and among them we created no small stir.

Several miles past Macclesfield we got a first sight of Bosley Cloud standing up in its comfortable sort of way, like an overgrown schoolboy among infants. Having made good time we reached Bosley Top Lock by 7 o'clock and so did not stop but went down the locks and were through the last one – number twelve – by 9.30 p.m., when we put up the cover of the *Hebe* and snugged down for the night.

We had chosen a spot for mooring just at the end of the aqueduct over the River Dane, and before darkness had finally settled, a young fellow came over the footpath and was going to pass us with a 'good night', but stopped out of curiosity and made a few envious enquiries as to our mode of holidaying. He himself was wont to camp during weekends on the banks of the river below us. At this time he was rather concerned over some of his property which he left in his (permanent) tent. This week he had returned to find a lot of it stolen. Somebody had evidently taken to robbing tents, for half a dozen others had been visited by thieves during the week.

Eventually as it grew darker our friend wished us good night and, after informing us of the lovely things he was going to cook for his supper, went off singing in order to keep up his spirits.

SUNDAY 11TH AUGUST

We woke to find a cloudy sky, and during breakfast – which meal we had in the shelter of the boat – there were a couple of sharp showers. The rain did not last long, however; the delay was quite trivial and we were soon away.

From here on, the canal banks were crowded with fishermen. Every few yards could be seen the figure of a disciple of Izaak Walton[1] placidly sitting over a rod and visibly thinking it would be better to have a little less sun. At least the fishing here seemed to have some element of fish about it for quite a number of anglers had specimens.

Handel Hall was apparently occupied. Indeed, it looked as if someone with an interest in the old place was living there. The whole house and garden seemed to be in better condition and the water lily pond made the scene lovely. At Hall Green the lock was indeed a lock – it was locked up! Only one gate was locked, so with care and circumspection we managed to squeeze the *Hebe* past and into the chamber.

From here to Kidsgrove is only a short mile, but as there is more or less a continuous line of locks from Kidsgrove to Middlewich we decided to have dinner first and then tackle them. A shady bank was soon found and approving of it we drew in, and soon the last of the cold chicken with which we had started out was but a pleasant memory.

The canal took a good turn just about here and the wind was brought directly astern. So we spun along into Kidsgrove, followed at a little distance by a score or so of the juvenile population who were hard put to keep up with us, so well did the wind blow.

Turning at right-angles again into the Trent and Mersey Canal brought the wind ahead, but this was not a matter of much concern as we were almost on top of Plant's Lock.

The lock keeper, a retired boatman and an old acquaintance of ours, completely won our hearts by running to prepare the lock for our entry, and many were the protestations of joy and friendship on both sides.

'Well well, as Ah said to the missus when Ah see'd yer sail round the corner, it's the old gentleman again in his boat. How are yer sir? Ah'm reet glad to see thee again.'

'Here! Not so much of the old gentleman about it!' was the Commander's reply.

---

1. Izaak Walton (1593–1683) was the author of *The Compleat Angler* (1653).

'And where are ye for this year guv'nor? What – *Nottingham*? Well thee's come wrong road for Nottingham. Oh ah! The tunnel's[2] shut up a'reet on Sunday. So thee's going through Middlewich eh? Ah know all the canals. Thee'll be going through Autherley and Great Haywood. All the same it's t'wrong road for Nottingham. All right. All right. I'll open the gates for ye.'

And with so many willing hands straining at the beams we made triumphant exit from Plant's Lock, providing the population of Kidsgrove with a topic of conversation for some time.

Originally we had intended to stop short of Middlewich, but although the wind was against us we made excellent progress, and as the evening was beautifully calm and clear we were on top of Middlewich before we knew it. Accordingly there rose the question: should we go on and push through Middlewich which meant nearly two miles and down three locks and on a mile or two more, or should we stop rather early in the evening? Eventually, after wasting nearly half an hour looking at the question from all angles, we decided in favour of going on. Taking short spells at the oars we sent the boat along to such good purpose that we overheard a remark in one of the locks: 'You'd be surprised how fast you can go in one o' them things.'

It was fairly dark by the time we had got through King's Lock and quite dark when we reached anchorage on a little bank about a mile along the Wardle branch, a little way above the second lock.

MONDAY 12TH AUGUST[3]

The sun was shining gloriously from a cloudless sky, and helped by a pleasant breeze we soon had the dew dried from the covers. But just as we were thinking how dry it was, that same playful little breeze got under the cover and lifting it up deposited it in the water. No harm done, but the cover was quite damp and had to be spread out to dry.

While this process was going on we were joined by the owner of the neighbouring fields, a farmer ready and eager for conversation. He gave us long dissertations on railways and roads and even the latest cotton prices. He had taken to the wrong calling. The man should have lived in Manchester and sold stocks, dealt in shares, or for a change floated companies, instead of rusticating on a farm in the heart of rural Cheshire.

---

2. Harecastle.
3. This would have been his twentieth birthday.

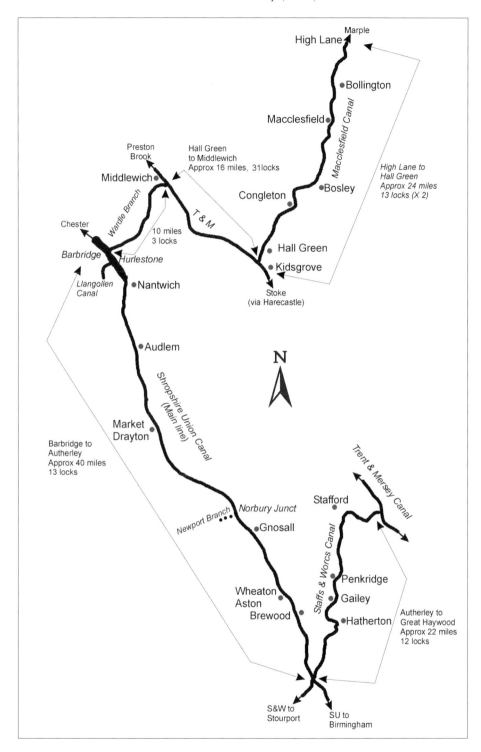

High Lane to Great Haywood, via Autherley.

The would-be financier gone and the cover dry, we made haste to pack up and get away. The wind was fairly strong and against us, so the Mate elected to tow.

The country through which we were now passing was that luscious, luxuriant green, characteristic of Cheshire, and with a bright sun and a blue sky flecked with great white cumuli the landscape was perfect.

Our quiet reflections were shattered by a motor barge heralding its advent while still far off. We were aware of its coming some time before it appeared, dragging behind it as usual a butty boat. Shades of the Eighteenth Century. What would Brindley have said or thought had he seen his canal churned by the screw of one of these oil-driven racket boxes? Brindley, who built the Wardle Canal, was responsible for the large-scale introduction of canals and might be thought the father of the English system.

At Church Minshull our diminishing store of food was replenished and we made a halt for dinner not far from the bridge. We chose a spot at the top of one side of a grassy hollow, and while having dinner the Commander spied something on the other side of the hollow. When we had finished he wandered over, and finding his suspicions correct, stooped down and picked our first mushroom. It was the only one thereabouts, for although the Mate searched diligently his efforts were not crowned with success. It served, however, to stimulate our interest, and during the rest of the voyage we managed to collect a great number of the fungi.

In spite of the breeze, which was quite stiff and against us for the present – a fact for which we were later to be grateful – we made good progress and by about two o'clock we reached Barbridge.

Barbridge is really just a few houses. The important thing to us was that here the Wardle Branch joins the Shropshire Union Canal. We had a long way to go along the Shropshire Union, and after the turn at Barbridge the wind, instead of being persistently against us, was now in our favour for many miles.

The canal is very wide here, and in one pool were a couple of swans. Taking fright at our sail they fled before us. Sticking to the water they kept ahead for seven or eight miles, the only reason that they turned back was because we came to a lock.[4]

While passing under one bridge not far from Nantwich we heard someone talking, and looking up saw two natives gazing earnestly down at us while one remarked to the other: 'Eh! I'll bet they're Scouts from the Jamboree.'

At Nantwich we called a halt for tea, and while the Mate made the preparations the Commander went into the town on the usual errand of buying food.

---

4. Most likely Hack Green Lock(s), Nos 28 and 29, about 6 miles from Barbridge.

The evening was glorious. A gentle breeze, not enough to disturb the reflections, moved us along through the water. The sky was almost cloudless, just a few flecks here and there broke with their many colours the lovely blue of the heavens. The canal banks were deserted and, beyond the occasional creak as a rope tightened when the zephyr stirred our white wings, everything was silent. Even the rabbits and birds were not disturbed by our coming, only looking up in mild astonishment as we slipped by. At times we passed a new-mown hay field and our nostrils were assailed by the intoxicating medley of scents only found at such places. Or perhaps it would be a field of meadowsweet tinging the air with its heady perfume. Once a heron slowly flapped its way along the sunset path. Occasionally an inquisitive horse would prick its ear and stroll down to the water to watch us out of sight.

Then, as daylight gave way to dusk, a rustle in the dry grass would tell us of some little animal coming out to feed, and a soft plop in the water would warn us of some vole going home. Over all brooded a heavy silence through which the *Hebe* floated like some magical barque.

Soon it became too dark to go any further. The lengthening shadows had warned us to moor for the night some time past, but the evening had held us enchanted and we could not break the spell. We stopped for the night not far from the little village of Audlem, and after supper as we were sitting in the boat a gentleman farmer appeared on the other bank. He was going to pass on but stopped out of curiosity and, after inspecting us, broke out with an incredulous, 'D'ye sleep in that thing?'

The Commander pointed out it was a nightly occurrence for us.

'I wouldn't dream of doin' it. Why, I haven't slept away from home for ten years or more.'

Having thus been introduced to the Commander he got into conversation. Soon it appeared they were almost old friends. The Commander and he had been born in Birmingham. They had even fished the same canal. The Commander had been to the same school, as had our friend's brothers. So naturally it was a little late by the time we turned in and the rabbits were scurrying and scuttering in the darkness of the shady bank.

TUESDAY 13TH AUGUST

Mushrooms for breakfast and once again we enjoyed the full flavour and soft meatiness of the fungi. The wind had changed during the night and was now blowing steadily ahead. However, the sun was shining brightly and had only a short way to go before meeting the first of the flight of fifteen locks at Audlem.

Early in the morning. Given the type of bridge in the background, this picture (from an original glass negative) was probably taken on the Trent and Mersey Canal, up from Middlewich.

Audlem is a typical Cheshire village, the biggest house being that owned by our acquaintance of the night before. There is an occasional butcher, likewise an occasional doctor and dentist. On the whole, life is very placid, mild excitement being caused by Johnny Smith's cut finger, and the arrival of a new inhabitant causing wild turmoil.

By 11.30 we could congratulate ourselves on having put the locks behind us. The top lock lies just at the entrance to a long vaulted avenue of trees. On emerging from this tunnel we were threatened with a shower and thought it best to take advantage of the shelter of the trees, so we put back a little way.

The rain having cleared away for the time being we left the shelter and were soon making good progress with the Commander on the towrope. While engaged in this pursuit he was looking over a field as the canal went along an embankment and spied something white glistening in the grass. So when the boat had stopped the Mate ran down the bank, over a hedge, and was rewarded by finding a tremendous mushroom. It was a really big beauty, freshly grown and weighing about a quarter of a pound, measuring six or seven inches across in its socks. After this, of course, a good lookout was kept

Audlem locks, from an
original glass negative.

and finally we came to a field with a plentiful crop. We had just picked a nice
quantity when the rain came on and we made a swift run for a bridge. Here
we stayed for an hour or so until the rain had stopped, and when it cleared
up we went on past Market Drayton.

Three or four miles past Market Drayton we came to Tyrley. Here the
canal narrows so much that we were forced to tow. After the fifth lock at
Tyrley the banks rise much higher. In places they are a hundred and fifty feet
high, crossed occasionally by a web-like bridge. Here and there the rock face
is quite bare but for the most part Nature has clothed the rock with trees
and bushes which cling to invisible cracks and sprout from invisible crannies
turning the cutting into a green valley.[5] Originally the naked face must have
been an eyesore but now on a summer's day it was a miracle of green leaves
with sweet little sighing airs ever moving among the branches.

---

5. My own memories of Tyrley in the 1960s are very similar, except that the towpath was
virtually non-existent and the canal badly silted. What I remember particularly were the
wild hops growing like great lianas over the jungle of trees.

Above and below: Two small commercial prints of Market Drayton.

Tyrely Cutting, from an original glass negative and partly restored.

It seems strange to us but in Brindley's time canals must have been ugly scars on the countryside. Now, after a lapse of more than a hundred years, they have so altered in appearance that they are delightful relics of the past, pleasing alike to mind and eye.

This cutting extended for two or three miles; it was so narrow that we were forced to tow. The sun was getting lower when we entered the cutting and we went through it at a fine pace. We emerged from this almost-tunnel to find the light very nearly gone and soon finding a grassy bank we pitched camp for the night.

WEDNESDAY 14TH AUGUST

The plentiful supply of mushrooms garnered the day before made a lovely dish. Then with the bright morning sun shining and the breeze urging us on we were soon speeding along, our white sails contrasting with the luscious green fields of Shropshire.

Once or twice we overtook or passed a milk boat. The firm of Cadbury have several barges on the canal engaged in carrying milk (brought down by farmers to the canal side) to one or other of two evaporating stations situated on this stretch of canal.

We had one adventure in the morning. Towards midday we had stopped for dinner and were engaged in picking mushrooms – of which there was a great number in this field – and had gathered a goodly few when a voice hailed us from the middle distance.

Turning we perceived a country bumpkin who proceeded to request us to remove ourselves. We at once complied, although this was the only time that anyone ever objected to our presence.

During this time a great number of boats kept passing. All went in the same direction and in order to avoid having to overtake them all we waited until what appeared to be the last to get ahead. Then, after giving them some time, we started. Our waiting, however, had not been to much avail, for in about half an hour the wind had brought us up to the tail-ender.

Now we were in a quandary. The wind was sufficient to send us along just a little faster than the barges, but hardly fast enough to warrant trying to overtake them. To use the oars at this time was rather against our principles, and so choosing the easier course we dawdled along for the best part of the afternoon behind the end boat.

The country on each side was charming. Lush grass and green meadows stretched away to right and left, and in the distance rose the Welsh mountains all blue against the sky, with the Wrekin standing grim above the rest.

Several miles past Norbury Junction and still a few hundred yards from the last boat we came to a tunnel.[6] The Mate went ashore to tow through and we observed that great interest was being taken in us by a gentleman with two small daughters and a dog, the last three gazing in astonished bewilderment. The Commander, whose turn it was to be lazy and lie in the boat, out of the goodness of his heart and regardless of the Mate, offered the family party a trip. They seized the chance with alacrity, stepped aboard and off we went, the Commander being bombarded with questions. Where had we come from? Where were we going? How long had we been out? Did we sleep on board? Did we drink canal water?

On entering the Stygian blackness of the tunnel excitement rose to fever pitch and many were the tales of adventure to be related to Mother. It appeared Mother was out for the day and Father was looking after the children. This perhaps explained their presence on the canal bank, Father in a pair of recently white (but no longer) shoes, daughters in frocks delightfully stained with assorted fruit juice and minus shoes and stockings.

We proceeded thus for a mile or so until it became evident that we were getting far from home and that our passengers must either turn back or keep going on and on with us. They decided to turn back. As they stepped ashore the head of the family asserted that having for the last three years contemplated the purchase of a boat he now intended to get one as soon as possible. So after a little discussion on the glorious delights of the water we left him a confirmed boating enthusiast.

The evening was as fine as the day had been. The wind had dropped and the reflections on the water were perfect as we pushed our way through a marvellous stillness that was almost alive.

Later, however, it grew cooler, especially when we went between the high pine-covered banks near Wheaton Aston. Accordingly we quickened our pace and were soon swinging along well. As was inevitable we caught up the barges. Feeling full of energy we decided to pass them, and getting out the tow rope we spent a strenuous half hour in that activity.

Passing through Brewood, with its church so prettily set among the trees, we swung along, and by the time it was almost dark we found ourselves at Autherley Junction. It thus became imperative to find a stopping place and eventually we came upon a convenient spot behind a barn. The Mate's log book shows we had made an excellent run of twenty-three miles.

---

6. Probably Cowley Tunnel, 81 yards in length.

Chapter II

Autherley to Great Haywood

THURSDAY 15TH AUGUST

As if to reprove us for thinking that this canal was losing its traffic, barge after barge went by while we were breakfasting. Some of the boats that we had overtaken yesterday now caught up with us and expressed their astonishment at the distance we had made the night before.

A start was made about nine-thirty and we made use of the few desultory puffs of wind to get to Autherley. This is the junction of the Shropshire Union Canal with the Staffordshire and Worcestershire Canal. Years ago the *Hebe* came along this route and turned to the right and reached the port of Gloucester. This time we would turn left and go towards Stafford.

The old lock keeper distinctly remembered the *Hebe* coming through his lock before, and was soon in deep conversation with the Commander who was turning the lock. As is often the case with end locks the difference in water levels was a matter of a few inches. As a result the actual rise and fall of the water is barely noticeable and unusually the filling of the lock takes longer than expected. However, after the water had been running out for about ten minutes the Mate became suspicious and took a look round. Immediately he began to chuckle with amusement and contemplated with delight the picture of the Commander and the lock keeper sitting absorbed in small talk while as fast as the water emptied from one end of the lock more water filled it from the other!

There are no shops at Autherley and we had to go about a mile in the Worcester direction as far as Tettenhall, a suburb of Wolverhampton whose racecourse we skirted along the way.

Beside this stretch of canal between Autherley and Tettenhall is a long row of boathouses. On the water were quite a number of pleasure boats making

Thought to be Autherley Junction, from an original glass negative and partially restored.

us feel Triton-among-minnowish. If they only knew who were were, thought we, they would surely greet us with a brass band.

Having restocked we set out, passing Autherley and entering a ten-mile pound which soon became very narrow. The canal had been cut through solid rock. In places it was made broader to allow two boats to pass. At one time we met one of the numerous canal boats that run here and had to retrace our footprints until we met a broad passing place.

'How far ye goin'?' asked the bargee.

'About twenty miles today,' answered the Commander.

'Ye'll be goin' up the locks then. Have ye got a windlass?'

'Oh yes. We'll be all right. We've come through a hundred or more. By the way, is there a tap further on?'

'No I don't think so.'

'What? No tap? What's happened to 'The Anchor'?'

'Oh ah. There's a tap there. I was thinking ye meant a water tap.'

'So did I, but we can use the other one too.'

And after bidding each other good day we went on. The day was very hot and we were continually on the lookout for barges and for safety places, so by the time we reached 'The Anchor' its cider had become nectar. 'Heavenly nectar' according to the Mate.

Further on we met a strange phenomenon. A pleasure barge. It resembled the boats in which Kings and Queens were wont to sail the Thames. Much shorter than a commercial barge it had very nice lines and was fairly high in the water. Amidships was an elaborate cabin and forward and aft were promenade decks. The whole was beautifully painted in white, picked out here and there with black and gold. There was no engine and the boat made good progress towed by a large horse.

Painted on the bows of this wonderful craft was the name *The Lady Atherton*, and we learned some time later that it belonged to Lord Atherton, the coal owner. We wondered which of the gentlemen lolling on the poop was the owner. If we had known we might have thanked him and commended him for not fitting a motor – anathema of your real boatmen.

This stretch of canal, which originally connected Autherley with Stafford via the Sow, is not nearly so busy as the same canal below Autherley and on to Worcester.

Nevertheless it is well kept and in good order. The countryside is charming, the canal meandering through it in a way altogether delightful, so gentle and aimless it appears to be.[1] The locks are a bit stiff but they enhance the natural beauty of the scene with fern-bearing gates and moss-covered stones, from the crevices of which spout countless little streams of crystal water.

At Gailey the lock bears at least the appearance of importance. Beside the lock there are two houses and a bridge. The lock house itself is a type of architecture unlike any other. To begin with the walls have no angles at all – the house is quite round. It is frequently whitewashed and this, in conjunction with the castellated walls, makes it an astonishing sight.

The lock keeper and his wife obligingly posed for a photograph and chattily informed us that people came from miles and miles to look at the house. We inquired of them if there was a pillar box or a post office in the neighbourhood and were told there was a box just across the road. Accordingly, having written a postcard or two, we went across the road to post them. Looking to see if we were in time for the night collection, under the heading of 'Hour of Next Collection' were the words 'Next Friday'. Just

---

1. The Staffordshire and Worcestershire is a contour canal engineered by James Brindley as part of his 'Grand Cross' scheme. It opened in 1772.

Above left: The lock keeper and his wife pose for a photograph at Gailey lock.

Above right: Gailey lock, with its unusual circular lock house.

that: next Friday. It epitomises the whole life on the canal and connections. Life goes on so slowly and so peacefully that there is no need for hurrying to post a letter. One has a week to write a letter and there is no likelihood of anything of such importance happening that a message must be despatched immediately.

Locks after this were fairly simple and all single. They did not involve any particular strain in passing.

Towards nine o'clock it grew dark, and just after passing a lock with a crowd of curious young people particularly interested in our progress, and finding ourselves in the lee of a great wood which stretched over each side of the canal, we stopped for the night.

FRIDAY 16TH AUGUST

On waking we found we had chosen for our camp a beautiful spot in a lovely park, which the sun shining its best made into a marvellously English landscape.

We made an early start and at once plunged into the gloom of the great wood. The silence in the trees was deep and the gentle plash of the oars was the only sound. The dip of the blades in the clear water makes an enchanting noise, especially among the great trees. The motion of a boat is devoid of any sensation of movement, and the sound of the oars with the occasional low stir of branches moved by a ripple gives one the impression of unreality as a dream. It has a touch of the lotus about it, for it imparts a pleasant kind of intoxication that, once enjoyed, is never forgotten.

The locks were still the lovely grass-grown mossy affairs of the night before and the countryside, baking in the sun, was in an idyllic mood.

Towards midday we passed a salt works[2] and just beyond it came to a canal junction.[3] Imagine a letter 'T' laid on its side. We had just come along one arm of the top of the 'T' (from the lower end) and wanted to go straight on across the top, which led to the River Sow. If we had got onto the river we could have gone on to Stafford. We had, however, to turn and go along the tail of the 'T' to Great Haywood.

At first we thought it might be possible to force our way through the reeds and get down to the river lock, then push through more reeds to the river which was only a hundred yards away. But on inspection we found the lock to be impassable. Having pushed and pulled our way to the lock our hopes were dashed. The upper gate was holding water and standing the strain very well, but the lower gates were only just moveable due to accumulated silt. Great gaps and rents showed in the planking. These alone would have stopped the lock filling, but also the boards were in the last stages of decay and in all probability would have given way if we had tried to fill the lock.

After a short consultation we decided against making a portage. There were only two of us to carry the boat, and so we changed our plans and turned our prow towards the Trent and Mersey Canal and set out for Nottingham.

By the time we had emerged victorious from a second struggle with the weeds it was nearly time for dinner and as the sky was threatening to deluge us with rain we made for the next bridge and took our repast in safety.

Just at our back was the old LNWR main line and during our stay at this spot we were entertained by a spectacle of many of the high flyers. The *Manxman* whistled by, shortly followed by the *Welshman* and after that thundered past the *Irish Mail*.

---

2. Baswich Bridge and Salt Works.
3. This would have been the junction with the River Sow Navigation. Bradshaw's canal handbook (1904) calls this Baswich Lock and gives a distance from there to Stafford Wharf of one mile. It is not mentioned in Imray's 1950 guide.

Ingestre.

During the afternoon the sky gradually became blacker and at about four o'clock we had to shelter under some trees and watch the drops falling into the water from the bushes. If we kept still an occasional water vole would paddle across the canal and inspect the *Hebe* with beady eyes.

After about an hour and a half we moved on although the rain was still gently falling. It is only in towns, among pessimists, that rain is depressing. All one has to do in the country when it rains is to accept it in a philosophical manner and it immediately becomes a vastly humorous business. The countryside takes on a different look, and with the rain comes that lovely rich smell of warm wet vegetation with its hundred and one tangs of the earth.

With the covers raised and our mackintoshes donned we towed the *Hebe* through a pleasant – albeit moist – country. At Milford the canal crosses the River Sow and we again discussed the possibility of navigating the river. At this point the river is quite deep and broad enough for the *Hebe* so we almost launched on the running water. When, however, we remembered the weather had been dry for the last three weeks and the river was probably very shallow in other places we decided to stick to the canal.

Towards seven o'clock the fury of the elements abated and shortly afterwards we began to look for a stopping place. In half an hour or so we neared a place where the canal opened out to nearly two hundred yards broad.[4] The bank opposite the towpath sloped in the form of a gentle lawn for a good half mile.

---

4. Tixall Wide.

At the top of the lawn stood Ingestre Hall, a noble house belonging to the Earl of Shrewsbury and Talbot. Hoping the aforesaid Earl had no objections, and not caring if he had, we moored on his lawn.

The mere was teeming with wildfowl which, after inspecting us and deciding we had no murderous intent, emerged from their rushes and scuttled about on the all-important business of food. The number of birds could not be counted but we made out no less than eleven different varieties.

The Earl seems to be a cattle fancier, for the fields were full of lovely beasts and some very fine calves came down and showed great curiosity towards the *Hebe*.

Chapter III

Great Haywood to Shardlow

SATURDAY 17TH AUGUST

The chattering of the many water birds woke us early to find the promise of a perfect day. Old Sol was doing his best but a steady breeze just right for sailing tempered his fire. The country round Ingestre bore the hallmark of rural England. The grass was a luscious green, the oak trees were real trees and not stunted dwarves struggling for existence, the fields were full of flowers, boundaries were known not by cold granite but by fat green hedgerows in which a multitude of sparrows, robins, finches and others chattered and sang. It was Arcadia.

We made an early start and were soon bowling along towards Great Haywood with the wind astern and blowing well. We kept up a good pace until after a couple of miles we got into the lee of a wood and had to take to the oars. Fortunately this was not for long as very soon we reached Great Haywood.

The barrier across the canal had not been opened since Friday night and we had to wait for an ancient mariner to come running out to let us through. This was the junction of the Staffordshire and Worcester Canal with the Trent and Mersey Canal. The latter we had joined near Harecastle and left at Middlewich, so we had made a great detour wandering around Cheshire and Shropshire to do it.

After passing the barrier and getting onto the Trent and Mersey it occurred to the Commander that it would be interesting to know how far we were from Burton on Trent. Turning about he addressed the deaf old gate keeper:

'How far is it to Burton?' in a loud voice.

'Wheer?' came the answer. 'Preston? Oh ah don't rightly know how far to Preston.'

'No Burton. BURTON.' In a still louder voice.

'Burslem?' From the ancient. 'Well now let me see … 'bout eighteen mile.'

'No. You delightful old man,' shrieked the Commander getting impatient. 'Burton. *Burton*, where the beer comes from.'

'Oh, beer. Well why didn't you say Burton. Well it's about nineteen miles. Good mawnin'.'[1]

Then as we settled into our stride a little boy appeared on the towpath and ran along keeping up with us, the while he volunteered screeds of information on the locality.

Almost immediately we came to the lock at Great Haywood, and while passing through we noticed several people with weird blue clothes with red ribbons and carrying long poles. The lock is almost under a little bridge and in the middle of a wood. As we passed out from the bridge we heard a great barking. The little boy became excited and enlightened us as to the meaning of all this.

'Ooh. Rotter'ounds. Rotter'ounds.'

Going up to investigate we found he was right. A meet of the Staffordshire Otter Hounds was taking place. Shortly afterwards they moved off along the banks of the River Sow, which hereabouts was very beautiful. Following their example the Commander moved off into the picturesque village of Great Haywood for provisions. On his return we hoisted sail and left there at a spanking pace.

The canal meandered through the countryside in a pleasant and intriguingly careless manner. At times the water was overhung by great beech trees, through the branches of which the sun filtered and flecked the water with a thousand golden patches. Occasionally the trees opened out and gave us a passing glimpse of the beautiful hall at Shugborough, shining white like a fairy castle in the sun. At times the gentle River Sow approached and seemed to invite us to launch on her limpid waters. The willows soughed in the breeze and appeared to be throwing up their leaves in shocked astonishment at our advent. The willows were always ladylike creatures, ever whispering among themselves and ready to weep at the slightest provocation. They set their roots in the bank and dip their leaves into the water, preening themselves and admiring their beauty in the river. As we passed we wondered if anybody lived in this delectable land, and what they thought of the *Hebe* which was surely a strange sight.

Later in the morning we passed through the town of Rugeley where, we supposed in our honour, the flags were flying and a brass band playing.

---

1. It is actually near enough 23 miles to Horninglow, but never mind.

Great Haywood.

Shugborough, from a contemporary postcard (see Plate 3).

Cannock Chase, Rugeley.

A contemporary postcard of Cannock Chase, Rugeley.

Making only the briefest acknowledgement of these courtesies we passed on and shortly after had to run for the shelter of a bridge to get out of the way of a shower.

After that we decided to have dinner, during which a bell ringer dolefully tolled his bell for a funeral. This not a whit affected our appetites and we made a royal repast of sausages, so proud in the knowledge of their excellency that in spite of the Commander's prodigious pricking they swelled and swelled and burst their golden skins with a hissing and crackling.

In the afternoon we sped gaily on our course, occasionally meeting a lock, or near Barton under Needwoood where we met a string of them. In one big pound we came upon a fishing competition and, *mirabile dictu*, the wind, instead of dropping, freshened considerably. We passed the competition with such a speed as to leave a lasting impression on the minds of the locals.

A catastrophe happened at Barton under Needwood. As is frequently the case, a bridge stands just beyond the lower gates of the lock. The bridge here is lower than the standard. Of course, there were half a dozen sightseers. The Mate was working the lock while the Commander looked after the boat. All went well until, the gates having been opened, the *Hebe* was gently gliding out and gathering way under the fierce arm of the Commander. The mast was stepped and as the bows got under the bridge there was a sudden jarring and scraping and the *Hebe* was quickly brought to a standstill with the mainmast jammed perilously under the bridge. To go either forward or backward in this state was impossible. We were stuck. Something had to be done at once. So in an effort to get the *Hebe* further down in the water at the bows the Commander ran forward. The Mate jumped aboard right forward, even forward of the mast, and grasping the 'stick' threw his weight to starboard and almost put the *Hebe* on her beam ends. With all these efforts the mast was brought just clear of the bridge and slowly, inch by inch, we gently slid into the open without apparent hurt.

Our congratulations were ill found for pride goeth before a fall. Three hundred yards from the scene of the accident a squall struck us and away overboard went the mainmast and the mainsail. After retrieving our damaged property, and with humiliation, we contrived to make considerable progress with the mizzen sail alone, and investigated the cause of the accident. This we found to lie in a broken step which, although broken at the bridge, had remained jammed until the squall struck and loosened the pieces.

A contemporary postcard of Barton under Needwood. The bridge shown is where the mast jammed.

At the next lock[2] the canal apparently made use of the river. The water was flowing at a good pace and the course turned and twisted in a way too great even for an English canal. The channel led through some very marshy ground and the towing path ran along a dyke which really consisted of a series of bridges running over little tributaries. With stream and wind so much in our favour we found before we knew it that we were in sight of Burton on Trent.

The town seen from the water looked rather straggling so we decided to stop for the night before going through. Accordingly we chose a grassy spot and were soon snugged down and all tight. While in the process of erecting the covers the Arm of the Law sauntered down the towpath, and after inspecting us decided we were quite harmless so entered into conversation with us by observing it was a fine night. After learning a little of our adventures he grew more and more enthusiastic about a holiday afloat and compared it with a holiday on the roads. He expressed abhorrence of the roads, their petrol engines and all that a petrol engine means.

SUNDAY 18TH AUGUST

We woke to find the sky gloomy and the rain so obviously near that we kept the covers up and had breakfast in their shelter. By the time we had finished, the rain had blown over and with the sun now shining we took down and packed away the covers.

We were now at no great distance from Shardlow and the terminus of the canal.[3] This being so we decided to push on, and at any rate try to reach the Trent if not Nottingham. Thus we did not linger and made an early start.

We had not gone a mile and a half before we were in Burton and among fishermen who stretched (one every 50 yards or so) so far along the canal that it was one o'clock before we saw the last of them.

While having breakfast a barge went by in the charge of a cheerful young fellow who inquired if we were going any further. We had given him the affirmative and now found that the locks, instead of being closed against us, were almost open for us. About ten o'clock we caught up with him (his name, we learned, was Matt Jones) and thanked him for drawing the upper paddles, promising to do the same for him as we passed through the locks.

---

2. The Trent and Mersey Canal enters and leaves the River Trent between Alrewas and Wychnor.
3. About 16 miles, but all the locks below Burton are broad rather than narrow.

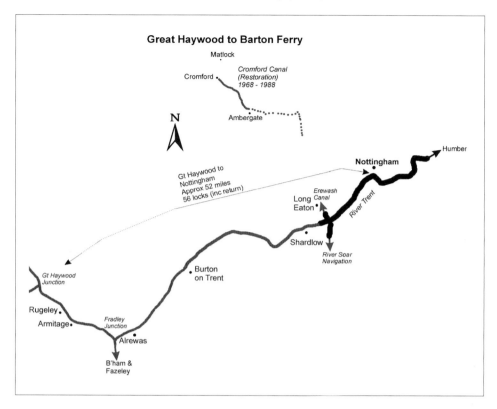

Great Haywood to Nottingham. For details of the Cromford Canal Restoration, see Simon Stoker, *There and Back Again: Restoring the Cromford Canal, 1968–88* (Amberley, 2008).

A contemporary postcard of Burton on Trent.

These locks now increased to double the normal width and could hold two barges instead of one.[4] With the increase in their size came an increase in the lack of oil and thus in stiffness.

Progressing gently though truly rural country we never seemed to get clear of the disciples of Izaak Walton. There are as many types of fishermen on the canal bank as there are fish in the water. The real old case-hardened fisher who has spent most of his life at the sport will hardly cock an eyelid as the boat goes by. In answer to a greeting he will ignore or give a non-committal grunt. The absolute novice, with rod in hand for the first time, will have his line out of the water and be warning his loud-voiced companions of your coming while the boat is still half a mile away.

Between these two extremes is a whole host of other types. There is the man who swears at you and, as once happened with the *Hebe*, declares that boats ought to be summonsed for being on the water at all. A more pleasant soul is his companion who cracks a joke and begs as a particular favour that you dip your oar deeper 'to stir 'em up, the lazy beggars'. There is the man who does not move until you are almost on top of him and, having to choose between running over his line or running ashore, you run over his line, he thinks unkindly of you. Besides these you often find wits who make reference to Volga Boatmen and other literary characters.[5]

Shortly after midday we came to a little bank which was clear of fishers, and seizing the chance we drew in. We found a shady little nook, and while preparing dinner a little girl sauntered down on the other side of the hedge and showed interest in us. She chattered gaily and after filling our can with water was delighted with a chocolate reward. Towards three o'clock with the sun shining brightly, as it had been all day, we set off again, still keeping ahead of Matt Jones.

Everything on and about the canal dozed in that peaceful atmosphere which is all that remains of another age. Occasionally we came in sight of a road with a superior air of detachment – the Sunday traffic tearing by – while the Commander related his experiences on one of the early motor cycles.

About six o'clock we arrived at the little village of Shardlow, ninety-three miles from Preston Brook, the far end of the Trent and Mersey Canal. On investigation we found two barges in the lock, and on the uppermost gates was a great padlock and chain which, we were informed, would not be removed until the next day, Monday, at 6 a.m.

---

4. To ADS, then used to the Macclesfield and similar canals, 'normal' would be 7 feet, so 14 feet in such a small boat would be quite a change.
5. Nothing much changes! He forgot to add the cretins who throw bait at you.

The *Hebe* is at times amphibious, but apparently not so at Shardlow. The lock keeper was a surly beast who assured us that the *Hebe* could not possibly get round the lock via the spillway. We discovered afterwards that he was frightened of what the bargees would say if we got past and they did not. On our return journey we found it would have been a simple matter to navigate the *Hebe* down the spillway.

Not knowing this at the time, however, we were forced to put back a little way and made camp about seven o'clock. An hour later when all was snugged down we were treated to a couple of heavy showers. It mattered not to us what the weather was doing, and having stopped early we turned in meaning to make an early start.

Chapter IV

The Trent

MONDAY 19TH AUGUST

In accordance with our resolution of the night before we were up early and with a calm air and a clear sky pulled away, and soon having passed the now opened lock we were on the last pound of the canal.

There was one adventure which must be noted which took place on this morning. As we were passing a derelict cart shed a hen, prospecting for dainties along the narrow ledge of the canal, took fright, and in trying to retreat fell into the water. Now the normal hen cannot swim and this was a distinctly normal hen. Quickly turning the boat, the Mate put all his weight into urging her forward. As we passed by the Commander, kneeling ready in the bows, leaned over, grasped the bird, and hurled it ashore just as it was about to sink for the third time. The Commander's zealous efforts were rewarded with an arm badly stung by a bunch of nettles which happened to be there. The hen, with an indignant cluck and a still more indignant glance at her tail which had suffered in the process, staggered off to her own barnyard.

The next lock[1] was not far away and on leaving it we were upon river waters.

Years ago the Commander related he had come with a friend up the Trent. They intended to take the canal at this point but the entrance was so hidden by reeds that they missed it. Their mistake was not discovered until they had gone several miles further up the river, and they only discovered their mistake when, going ashore to reconnoitre, they saw an old wooden bridge at the canal's entrance. Of this bridge more anon.

---

1. Derwent Mouth Lock. The first (or last) on the T&M.

Plate 1. L&NWR railway pass from 1922 in the name of Stephen Stoker.

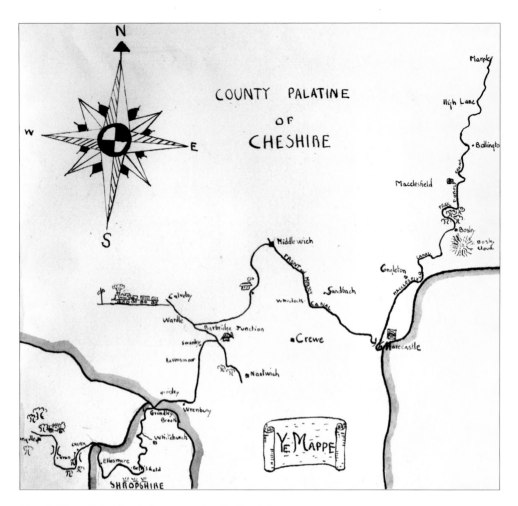

Plate 2. The original hand-drawn map for the first Adventure.

Plate 3. Shugborough, from a contemporary 'coloured' postcard.

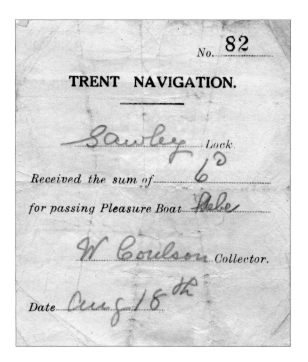

Plate 4. This pass took the Hebe through to Nottingham and back – about 22 miles for 6*d*.

Plate 5. Tug ticket for Harecastle. This took the Hebe three miles – it would have taken 30 tons of coal the same distance. 1*s* 3*d* is the equivalent of about £3.50 in 2011.

LONDON & NORTH EASTERN RAILWAY.

Plate 6. Permit dated 1 August 1930. Price 4*s* 10*d*.

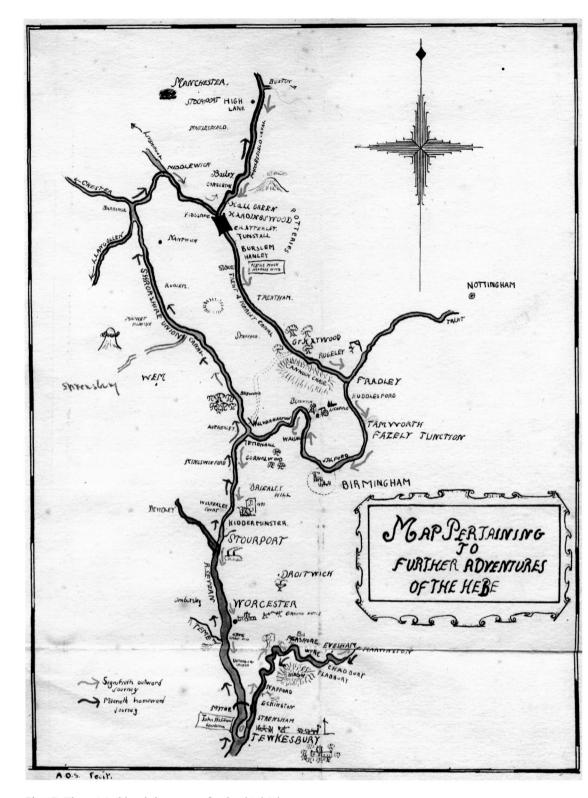

Plate 7. The original hand–drawn map for the third Adventure.

Plate 8. The turreted bridge. This picture was taken on a later trip in 1974.

Plate 9. A circular weir similar to the one described in Book Three. This picture was taken on a later trip in 1971.

Plate 10. Kinver, from a contemporary 'coloured' postcard.

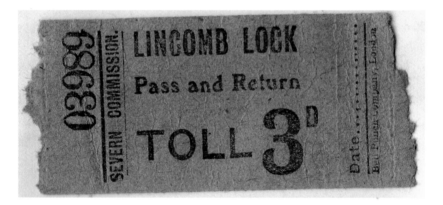

Plate 11. Ticket for the Lincomb Lock.

Plate 12. The Severn at Upton, from a contemporary 'coloured' postcard.

Plate 13. A modern view of Fladbury Mill, after the navigation was restored.

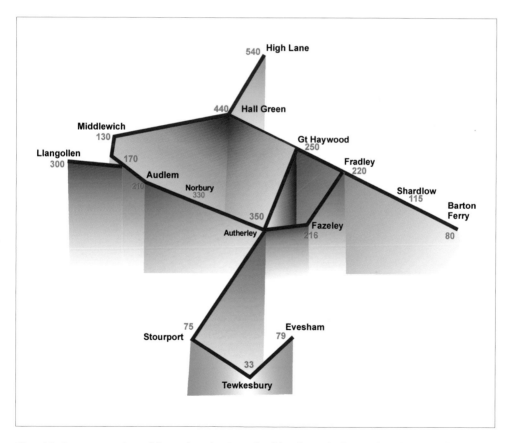

Plate 14. A representation of the various levels attained by the *Hebe* during the adventures featured in this book. The figures in red are approximate heights above sea level.

Monday 12th August.

The sun was shining gloriously from a cloudless sky, and, helped by a pleasant breeze soon had the dew dried from the cover. But just as we were thinking how dry it was, the same pleasant breeze in its playful little way, got under the cover and lifting it up deposited it in the water. No harm was done, but the cover was quite damp and had to be spread out to dry.

While this process was going on, we were joined by the owner of the neighbouring fields, a farmer ready and eager for conversation. He gave us long dissertations upon railways, and roads, and even the latest cotton prices. He had taken to the wrong calling. The man should have lived in Manchester, and sold stocks, dealt in shares, or, as an agreeable change floated companies, instead of rusticating on a farm in the heart of rural Cheshire.

The would be financier gone, and the cover dry we made haste to pack up and get away. The wind was fairly strong and being against us the Mate elected to row.

The country through which we were passing was that luscious, luxuriant green, characteristic of Cheshire, and with a bright sun and a blue sky flecked with great white cumuli the landscape was perfect.

Plate 15. A page from the original manuscript, which was handwritten with photographs pasted in.

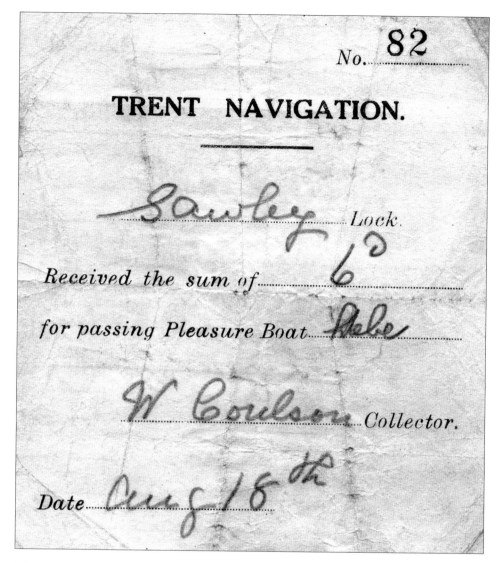

No. **82**

TRENT NAVIGATION.

———

Sawley Lock.

Received the sum of 6ᵈ

for passing Pleasure Boat Hebe

W Coulson Collector.

Date Aug 16ᵗʰ

This pass took the *Hebe* through to Nottingham and back – about 22 miles for 6*d* (see Plate 4).

Just now, however, the entrance was very clear and obvious. Traffic on this canal was increasing and we had been told by the last lock keeper that around ten thousand tons had passed up since March.

It is hard to describe the experience of leaving the confines of the canal and venturing for the first time in a long while on the broad expanse of a river, and just below Shardlow the Trent is very wide. We seemed suddenly to have shrunk to tiny proportions. Having been lords of creation on the canal

That 'rustic' bridge.

we were lost on the river, a change so sudden that it resembled abandoning ship in mid-ocean and taking to the boats. The waters, however, were calm, and we had no trepidation in venturing onto their wide surface.

Where the canal joins the river[2] the towing path is on the right bank and there is a bridge for horses to cross. On investigation this structure was found to be be in an advanced stage of decay. From a distance it seemed to be solidly built and supported on great wooden joists. These joists were, it is true, a little out of the perpendicular, but not enough to cause alarm. When we drew near, however, we found the reason some of the joists were out of the perpendicular was that they were actually swinging, tied by bits of old rope to the bridge. We could see no reason why the bridge should not fall down, but by exercising a little care we were able to cross it in safety.

At Shardlow we had been told it was only nine miles to Nottingham[3] and so decided to go there at once. A favourable breeze had sprung up and so with wind and water helping us we were soon speeding down the Trent.

We soon came to Sawley Lock and here, more than ever, the *Hebe* seemed lost. The modest sum of sixpence was demanded here for the distance to Nottingham, eleven miles we were told. We seemed to be getting further from, not nearer to, our goal but undaunted we held on.

---

2. In fact the T&M joins at the confluence of the Derwent, on the left, and the Trent which takes almost a right-angle path from the right. Modern aerial pictures show this bridge not to exist any more.
3. It is about 8.5 miles to the Beeston Cut and 11 or so miles to the middle of town.

Occasionally the river would take a turn so the wind came against us, and then we had some stiff work. We never seemed to be getting nearer Nottingham and as we wanted to have time in hand for the return journey we stopped at Barton Ferry, some four or five miles short of our destination.

Before we started on the homeward journey we thought it best to refresh the inner man, and selected a grassy bank to perform that operation. The Commander went off to Barton to lay in further stock and carried with him instructions from the Mate to buy a newspaper. In fact (and this is great testimony for a canal holiday) we had not seen a newspaper since our start over a week before. We had simply not been able to get one. We had started when a cotton strike was in progress and every now and then we wondered in a quiet sort of way what had been happening in that industry. However, when the Commander asked for a paper from the proprietor of the only store he got the answer, 'No, we haven't got a paper. You see it's Monday.' And then in a brighter tone: 'But we shall have one tomorrow. You can get Monday's paper on Tuesday,' suggesting by his tone of voice that if we really wanted to read a paper we wouldn't mind waiting a day.

The Commander having returned and dinner having been finished we turned the *Hebe* and set out on the homeward journey. The wind which had helped us so nobly before was now dead ahead and we soon took to the towline.

Barton Ferry, from a contemporary postcard. A steamer is clear on the mid-left.

After passing the beautiful boathouse at Cranfleet,[4] with its long row of sailing dinghies, we saw a boatbuilder's notice and pulled in to try for repairs to our broken mast step. The builder was a surly beast who would undertake nothing less than building a new *Hebe*, but we were directed to another man a little higher up who we were told could do the job for us. Rowing up the river we soon came to this man and repairs were put in hand.

The boatbuilder's assistant was astonished when he heard of the *Hebe*'s home port. He told us he was really down here on holiday helping his uncle but he was actually born and bred in Stockport.

We took tea at the boathouse but it was a cheerless meal. The windows of the restaurant were of frosted glass giving no view. The place was deserted and the boards, echoing hollowly under the feet of the solitary waitress, created an atmosphere in keeping with the emptiness of the fern baskets and the general draughtiness of the place.

It was but a short mile and a half to Shardlow, which village was soon passed (the Mate being taken as the Commander's man at the lock) and camp was pitched for the night eighty-nine miles from Preston Brook and five from Shardlow.

---

4. Cranfleet is, in effect, on an island formed by an 'S' bend in the Trent. On one side is the Cranfleet Cut – the short canalised section – and on the other the river bears right and then left over a weir. The River Soar arrives at that point and the Erewash Canal (Trent Lock) joins just above the Cranfleet Cut. It is quite a busy junction and a favourite with onlookers.

Chapter V

The Trent and Mersey

TUESDAY 20TH AUGUST

With plenty of time in hand and the sun shining as best he had done since the start, these factors combined to make our progress somewhat tardy, especially through the locks. At one of these big locks we met an interesting character in the person of an old man, originally the lock keeper, who although now retired was still living in the lock house and helping with the gates. It appeared he found time hanging on his hands now that he did not have to inspect the banks, and so to beguile his leisure hours had taken up reading. His favourite author was Bernard Shaw, and our lock keeper expressed emphatic agreement with him on many ideas.

After a long chat with the old man, who was delighted to have found someone who had heard of G.B.S., we reluctantly continued on our way. The canal here was very fine, with beautiful glimpses of the river being obtainable through the trees. This was especially the case near Weston where the meadows and the river were nearly on a level and with solemn herds of cattle standing knee deep in the water gently swishing their tails. The scene was one of enchanting rusticity. For the most part the birds were silent, only occasionally trilling a note which served to accentuate the deep silence pervading the countryside.

Towards eleven o'clock we seemed to be in the vicinity of a village. We distinctly saw two cottages and three people. The Mate went ashore to look around and returned with spoils of the earth. The weather was gloriously hot so that after dinner we were not exactly in the mood for strenuous work. Accordingly our progress was rather slow.

We managed, however, to reach Burton before nightfall and had an amusing experience as we passed through. The canal in one place runs by

Above: The Trent near Weston.

Left: A stopping place.

Burton church, from a contemporary postcard.

a playground which was filled with kiddies of all ages. Of course they had to run and watch us and then to keep alongside. In order not to disappoint the toddlers we had to proceed at about two miles an hour. By the time the end of the playground was reached at least half the population of Burton was following us and keeping up a conversation with the Commander.

It was fairly late by the time we got beyond Burton, so choosing a quiet spot we pitched camp for the night.

WEDNESDAY 21ST AUGUST

While preparing breakfast we were visited by a family comprised of Father, Mother, John and Peter. They lived in a house about half a mile along the canal and had come out on a tour of investigation, curious as to what our green cover was which had caught their eye the night before. After ten minutes' conversation they had to return as their breakfast was waiting, but not before we had promised to give John and Peter a ride when we went into Burton.

About nine o'clock John and Peter appeared again and were soon acquiring the art of rowing under the expert tuition of the Commander while the Mate was looking around Burton.

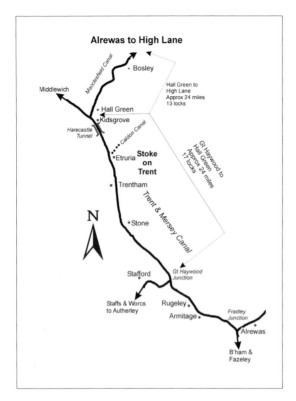

Alrewas to High Lane.

Burton on Trent may well be regarded as one large brewery. Everywhere, in every street, are breweries. Barrel makers are to be found here and there, likewise a shop or two, but in the main it is breweries. There is, however, a fine old Abbey and the River Trent itself is quite charming.

When we finally set out on our journey we carried not only Peter and John but also their mother who expressed a desire to take a trip. Father, of course, was away working in a brewery. We carried our passengers as far as the next lock where they bid us a reluctant farewell.

By this time it was nearing midday and after another two or three miles we drew in for dinner. While on the lookout for a comfortable spot, three goats joined us and made friendly advances. Indeed, they could hardly be persuaded to go home. They must have followed us for three miles or more.

In the afternoon the wind was against us and as the sun was hot we dawdled along. We soon approached the place where the canal and river are one. Here we made use of the great number of little bridges parallel to the canal which take the towpath over numerous tributaries flowing in to the river.

The locks were not infrequent and at one of them a party was picnicking. Learning that we were bound for Manchester one child of seven, or thereabouts, remarked, 'It'll be late when they get into Manchester tonight.'

In the evening, as the Commander was gently paddling the *Hebe* along, he cast his eye over a field and imagined he saw a mushroom. We landed to investigate but it turned out only to be a bit of paper. Our time had not been wasted, however, because on looking around we discovered the field was almost carpeted with mushrooms. It was the work of a moment to get various pots and pans and in a very short time we had collected between two and three pounds of beautiful fresh fungi. Just as we were setting out to fill the remaining pots and pans a lock keeper, who had come along the opposite bank on his way home, informed us that if we were to go on a little way and inspect another field which he indicated we would find much bigger and better mushrooms. We followed his advice, but although we looked long we looked in vain; there were none to be seen. But we had plenty so it was not important we found none.

It was now fairly late in the evening, so abandoning the hunt for mushrooms we hunted instead for a place to camp. This was easier said than done for the bank was too steep, or else it was too marshy and we had to keep on going until we came to a convenient spot. Eventually we reached a well-wooded bank and forced the *Hebe* through rushes to firm ground. We were none too early, for soon after the cover was up we heard the rain pitter among the leaves and splash into the water.

THURSDAY 22ND AUGUST

It was a glorious morning, and after a glorious breakfast of MUSHROOMS, MUSHROOMS, and bacon, we made a good start about ten o'clock. We were now running on a carefully thought-out schedule. The last ten miles of this canal (for us) runs through the Potteries. There is absolutely no place to camp and as the country is fearfully black we intended to reach its outskirts on Friday night and make a run straight through on Saturday. It was necessary to reach the end of the canal[1] before seven o'clock on Saturday night or else we would be forced to wait until Monday for a tug. Accordingly our progress had to be neither too fast nor too slow.

The stretch of canal upon which we were now sailing extended for ten miles without a lock and we therefore settled down to a leisurely time.[2]

---

1. Meaning the summit and Harecastle Tunnel. The junction with the Macclesfield Canal is at Hall Green on the other side of the tunnel.
2. Most likely this would have been the section from Wood End Lock, just above Fradley, to Great Haywood.

A contemporary postcard of the bridge at Great Haywood.

At one side the canal runs alongside a large-ish copse. In the middle of the trees stands a semi-clerical building, and as we passed by we observed what appeared to be a woman hanging out washing. The figure was dressed in a long white gown with a girdle round the waist, but there seemed something odd about the whole affair. A little distance further on and we saw another figure exactly the same and it all suddenly dawned on us that these were monks and the building was a monastery. It was thus with some curiosity that we took a look at this strange place. It was so much enclosed that it seemed entirely cut off from the outside world. We passed along its boundary, but for all we could make out we might just as well have been in Timbuktoo. So we cannot give a learned dissertation on the monastic system and must resist the temptation of talking about it.

At Rugeley it was market day. The open air market was a relic of the old days, even to the possession of a quack physician with his cure-alls and persuasive manner and loud convincing voice. His stock of remedies was rapidly diminishing and we passed on to the contemplation of a most marvellous collection of pies containing all the ingredients known to the culinary world. We could have bought steak pies, kidney pies, mutton pies, beef pies, steak and kidney pies and just plain meat pies. Again we resisted the temptation and instead bought three pounds of prime steak which was duly consumed at dinner time.[3]

For the second day in succession we managed to buy a newspaper but did not succeed in discovering whether the cotton strike was over. We came to the conclusion that either it was all over and done with or the newspapers had grown tired of reporting it. We found when we got home our first theory was the correct one.

The afternoon, like the morning, was absolutely cloudless. The sun beat down, bathing the country in a glorious light. The scenery was delightfully rural and everything was so peaceful that one could imagine it to be Arcady at least. Staffordshire is extraordinarily pretty in places.

We approached Great Haywood in the evening and suddenly, as we were nearing the lock, a shower of rain came tumbling down. It did not last long, and in half an hour or so the sun was shining again, quite his old self.

Having passed through the little village we were now on the lookout for a camping place and one soon presented itself. The cover was rigged and everything snug by about nine o'clock and bed.

FRIDAY 22ND AUGUST

The night had been wet, so accordingly we waited some time for the cover to dry in the sun before packing up. The wind was not in our favour and we had to do a lot of manhandling. Locks were not frequent but at one of them the Commander had an adventure.

We had risen to the top with the Commander in the boat and he was just about to step out and hand our water can to the lock keeper for a fresh supply. Suddenly the wind caught the *Hebe* and pushed her away from the wall, just at the moment when the Commander put his foot out of the boat. What exactly happened is unclear, but suddenly the Commander was kneeling with one leg in the *Hebe* and the other in the lock. The boat was leaning at an alarming angle but luckily did not capsize. Nothing worse than a wet foot resulted but naturally it provided food for conversation on the Mate's part who was thoroughly amused.

Our progress after this was not particularly fast. We spent our time towing and rowing. The country was not conspicuously beautiful – we were nearing the Potteries and occasionally would become aware of that fact.

---

3. Interestingly, he has here much later annotated the margin of the book with two large exclamation marks!!

We reached Trentham somewhere about eight o'clock. This is really the last rural part of this area. Accordingly we passed through the lock and pitched camp for the night. The lock keeper was an obliging sort of man and told us tales of the enormous quantities of mushrooms to be gathered in a field just off the towpath. The Mate went along just before supper and succeeded in gathering a few, not a great number but sufficient to add a pleasant flavour to our breakfast bacon and eggs.

SATURDAY 24TH AUGUST

We were awake right early. Today we had to make certain of getting through the tunnel at Harecastle and into the lovely country beyond. The Commander, ever the first to turn out, arose about seven a.m. Thinking that a few more mushrooms might be acceptable he set out in the direction of the same field. Hardly had he gone more than two hundred yards from the boat before a tremendous burst of rain came along, so hastily retracing his steps he was soon in the shelter of the boat and anxiously surveying the sky.

The weather clerk had indeed done us a dirty trick. Until now the sun had done his best for us every day, except for the occasional shower it had been continuously fine weather. This day, the only one in which we were forced to make a certain amount of progress, was wet. There was no break or lift in the clouds, as far as we could see it was one of great greyness. And all the time the rain came pouring down.

We had to have breakfast on board and afterwards sat in the shelter and watched the rain. Eventually, having gown tired of this occupation, we decided it was getting late and set off in spite of the wet. We took down the iron hoops which stretch the cover but left the cover itself lying over everything. Capes and coats and oilskins were donned, the towline was rigged, and we started on a dash through the Potteries. Ten miles to the tunnel and raining hard.

Words cannot describe that dash. Almost immediately we left the green and entered the black. We had gone less than two miles when we came to five locks in the middle of a town where we acquired an escort of grubby little boys all squelching through the mud after us and clamouring for a ride.

This country does a lot of canal trade. We met many boats laden with crates of earthenware or china clay. At Etruria the towing path is sometimes red but more usually white. There were so many boats tied to the wharves here that the Mate, who was towing, gave up in despair and took to the oars in spite of the discomfort of rowing in a coat.

For miles we did not see a decent clean blade of grass. Sometimes we would pass through pottery factories with crowds of potters at the doors and windows. At other times we would pass great gasworks and not see a soul. Only there would be clangings and little buckets on chains would climb into the sky, and now and then a tremendous rumble would be heard. If it were a little darker and there were a few more flames we might have been in the nether regions. Stoke on Trent is the dirtiest and most industriously horrible city on earth.

Two miles short of Harecastle we were about to overtake a barge when their steerer offered us a tow if we were going on through the tunnel. He himself was going for the next tug and would be delighted to tow us.

'Get thee in,' said he to the Mate. 'Get thee into boat out of rain.' And as he said so he caught our towline and made it fast.

It was about half past two when we eventually reached Harecastle and went in search of the tugboat man. We found him in his office which stands between the old tunnel[4] and the new. The old tunnel has no towpath and boatmen must push their boats through with their feet, a process known as legging.

The tug man was a round, cheerful-looking fellow who showed us where to get our things a little drier while waiting for the tug to start. He, meanwhile, went off to sell tickets to the bargees. On his return he gave us a hand lamp and a couple of lengths of wood with which to fend off the *Hebe* from the walls of the tunnel.

Promptly at three o'clock the procession started through the three-mile tunnel. In front was a motor barge, and after it came another barge bearing

---

4. Brindley's original tunnel was 2,880 yards with no towpath and constructed between 1770 and 1777. It turned out to be a bottleneck on the busy line and so a second ('new') tunnel was built by Telford, completed in 1827 and 2,926 yards in length. An electric tug ran in the second tunnel from 1914 to 1954. Both tunnels suffer from subsidence, and when I first went through in about 1960 the old tunnel's southern entrance was very low to the water and the tunnel was abandoned. The water on the Etruria side was bright orange due to the iron oxide being washed into the canal inside the tunnel. We hit the remains of the old towpath which caused a major leak on the front shoulder of our old wooden narrowboat and came out to Kidsgrove with one chine almost out of the water to stop it until repairs could be made.

    As a small boy I was left alone at the wharf in Middlewich (while my parents had to get home for a day or so) continually to pump out the leaking boat. Two old canal hands came along, took us down the next lock into a short pound, drained the whole lot and plonked the boat on the mud. Then they stuffed the rather large hole with oakum and nailed an aluminium patch over it! They never asked for payment.

    That boat, the *Stoke*, was never dry and the shoulders and most of the bottom plank were rotten. We never stopped pumping it out.

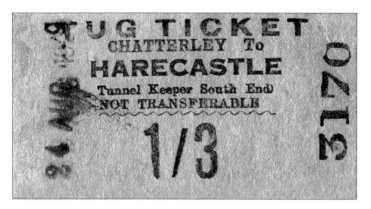

Tug ticket for Harecastle. This took the *Hebe* three miles – it would have taken 30 tons of coal the same distance. 1*s* 3*d* is the equivalent of about £3.50 in 2011 (see Plate 5).

a hundred and fifty accumulators for the motors. Then came eight or nine ordinary barges (at the other end of the tunnel fourteen were waiting for the return trip) and last of all the *Hebe*.

Our rate of progress was not excessive; an hour or so would be taken on the three miles. It was a new experience to be towed through the tunnel and one could almost feel the silence. The noise of the motor far ahead seemed so distant that one thought one was in utter silence. A slight glow came from the boats ahead, silhouetting the shoulders of the steerers. A boat far down the line would occasionally bump and that bump would pass from boat to boat. Sometimes a drip of water could be heard, otherwise there was silence and darkness. Absolutely no motion could be felt and it was only by turning the feeble rays of the hand lamp on the walls that we could see we were sliding along.

This went on it seemed for ages. At last we heard one of the diesel motor barges ahead kick up a row and knew the exit was near. A strange natural phenomenon was noticed as we came to the end. When the outer world became visible it had taken on a deep orange-yellow tint. On reaching the outer air this disappeared, but exactly what the cause was is a mystery.

As the boats left the tunnel the fat round boatman collected the tickets, but we handed in the lamp and thanked him, so he forgot to ask for ours and we kept it.

Our own canal was only just round the corner so we set out immediately. And immediately it rained as it had not rained before. A real 100% out and out downpour. It didn't make much difference to us as we were pretty wet already. However, we had not gone far on our home waters before the rain stopped and the sun shone out once more. We changed our clothes, bailed out the *Hebe*, had a whacking great meal of bacon and eggs and were at peace with the world.

SUNDAY 25TH AUGUST

As if to make up for the ghastly weather of the day before, the sun was once again shining with all its strength. The grass was greener than ever, the flowers were brighter, and everything was pleasant.

Just as we were preparing to cast off, our friend in the *Annie* caught us up, and to conform to standards of decency we let him go by and get into the locks which were all ready for the next boat to go up. After giving him about half an hour's start we again set out and being by far the speedier boat we passed him a couple of miles from Bosley Top Lock. The bargee, however, scores in the matter of speed by not stopping for meals. He may go slowly but he never stops from dawn till dusk. While we were having dinner not far from the Royal Oak he again passed us.

He had caught up while we were eating but in the afternoon we again caught up and passed him before Macclesfield. While going through this part of the world we passed another fishing competition. Not many anglers had any luck, and one said as he finished his mid-morning snack, 'Ah! That's the best bite I've had all day.'

Near the Royal Oak.

Above left: The beginning.

Above right: The end, 90 feet of towline and 70 feet of narrowboat later.

It was with great delight that we again viewed our old familiar haunts. We seemed to have been away for years, but now we were back again and pointing out landmarks to each other with the air of an industrial magnate visiting his childhood home.

We found our old picturesque wharf occupied by two motor boats and were horrified to see what their owners were doing. With great long rakes they were engaged in uprooting the glorious spread of water lilies which we were so careful not to harm. The *Hebe* glides over these beautiful plants but does not hurt them, but here was a crowd of vandals tearing them up to make room for their propellers.

We looked on more in sorrow than in anger. People, especially people with motor boats, when they hear that *Hebe* is man-powered suggest it would be better to have a motor fitted, and so be able to go further and be less tired and so on. Consider these facts:

The *Hebe* is about the only rowing and sailing boat on our canal. There are a score or more of motor boats. Yet if the total number of trips made by motor boats was found it would be less than one quarter of the trips made by the *Hebe* in one season. Only one motor boat of all this number has been beyond Bosley locks while the *Hebe* has been many hundreds of miles beyond them.

In the other direction the canal winds along the charming Goyt valley.[5] The motor boat owners know nothing of this lovely spot for their craft always run aground before they get there. As for the *Hebe* being more tiring – nonsense! Rowing is splendid exercise and we do not make it a toil. As for sailing, that is a delightful sport. On the other hand when a certain motor boat owned by a party of young men goes out, these young men can usually be seen playing cards as the boat goes along. With a boat like the *Hebe* one's interest is always occupied.

We leave you to judge which is the more pleasurable: the gentle *Hebe* or that racketing, noisome, stinking, quivering invention of Satan – the motor boat.

We did not stop for long at the wharf but hastened for High Lane. Arriving there we tidied and cleaned the gallant boat, who had stood us for so long, and reluctantly closed the boathouse door and departed for home.[6]

---

5. From Marple Junction to Whaley Bridge is the Peak Forest Canal.
6. As far as I can judge, this trip covered 212 miles and 161 locks.

HISTORICAL MISCELLANY
1930

6 March   Clarence Birdseye markets frozen peas for the first time

12 March   Gandhi starts the 'salt march' in protest at the British monopoly on salt. (He will be arrested a number of times throughout the year.)

24 May   Amy Johnson lands in Darwin, Australia, and becomes the first woman to fly solo from England to Australia.

16 August   British Empire Games held in Hamilton, Ontario.

21 August   Princess Margaret born.

24 September Noel Coward's play *Private Lives* first performed at the Pheonix Theatre, London.

5 October   The British airship R101 destroyed in an accident over France.

ALSO:

Sellar and Yeatman publish *1066 and All That*.

3M begins marketing Scotch tape.

Youth Hostel Association founded.

Pluto, the dwarf planet, discovered by Tomghaugh.

The Times publishes its first crossword.

Military coup in Peru. Revolution in Brazil.

The Nazi Party becomes the second-largest party in the Reichstag.

First World Cup in Uruguay.

BOOK THREE

THE FURTHER ADVENTURES OF THE HEBE
1930

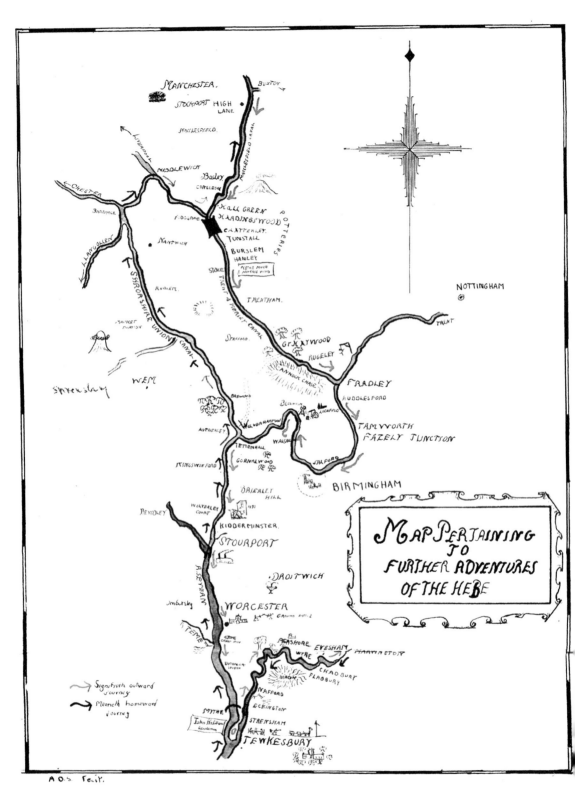

The original hand-drawn map for this book (see Plate 7).

Preface

Having made many attempts to write a preface, or an excuse for this little book, I have come to the conclusion that it is a feat beyond my powers.

However, there are just two things I would ask of anyone who flatters me by reading it. The first is that you should not take this as a faithful chronicle of all that occurred on this eventful voyage. The second is that before you start the first chapter you should take a glimpse at the map. If you do so I am certain you will understand the story much better.

By now I expect you are speculating whether or not to carry on, so I will hastily conclude and thank you for having paid me such rapt attention thus far.

ADS
1930

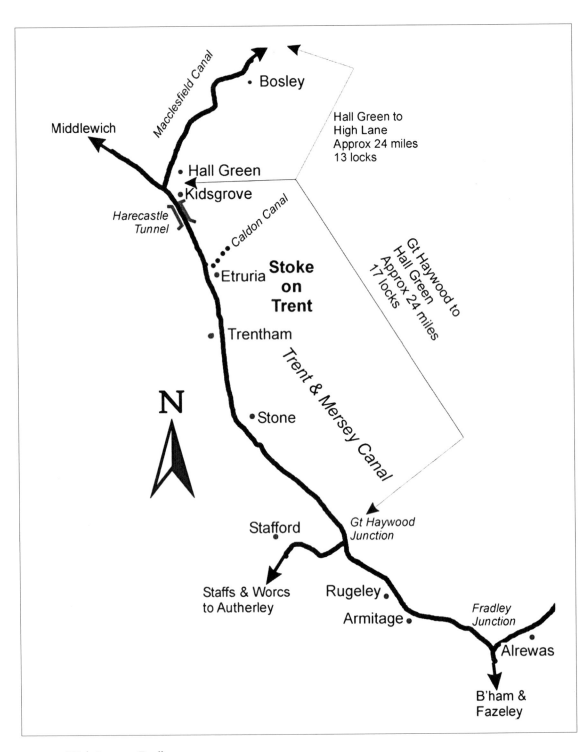

High Lane to Fradley.

Chapter I

The Macclesfield and the Trent and Mersey Canals

THURSDAY 31ST JULY

It was on a calm and Thursday evening in July when the *Hebe* set out on her voyage into the little-known regions of English canal land. Manned by two souls in all, her crew consisted of the Commander – so-called on account of previous navigational knowledge – and the Mate, as yet still a little new to this world of canals and boats and locks.

The first part of our voyage lay along the placid waters of the Macclesfield Canal 'which takes its course at a splendid elevation at the foot of the moors, through a most diversified and picturesque tract of country'. A blue haze spread itself over the great Cheshire plain and the county of the oak and the cornstook became a misty fairyland.

The evening being windless we made no use of our sails, but paddled along gently past Bollington and through Macclesfield, overtaking two canal boats near the latter. They were preparing to stop for the night so we got out the towrope and soon were leaving them far behind. At one likely little farm we went ashore and got into conference with the farmer's wife regarding eggs, while her dog raised the neighbourhood with his barking, so surprised and indignant was he at the sight of the *Hebe*. Business completed we resumed our progress for a mile or so, pitching camp just before reaching a hamlet which goes by the delightful name of Fool's Nook.

FRIDAY 1ST AUGUST

Next day, Friday, dawned with the promise of fine weather. We were awake early, being brought back to consciousness by the sound of a gun, and, while

Hebe under sail,
most likely on the
Macclesfield Canal.

dressing, a burly farmer with gun and dogs appeared on the towpath. He was, he said, out for anything, and had already killed half a dozen water hens.

Whether he did it on purpose or not we never found out, but shortly afterwards we heard a shot, and in the silence that followed were startled to find the bullets pattering on the canvas cover of the boat. Luckily they were spent by the time they reached us, but as he said he was out to shoot anything we wonder if possibly we were included in that morning's bag.

We soon polished off breakfast and set out on our second day's voyage. Forty minutes or so brought us to the top lock at Bosley. Luckily all the locks were in our favour and we had passed the whole twelve a little after eleven o'clock. The wind was now in our favour, and being a little tired after the unaccustomed exercise of the locks, we hoisted sail and drew away from Bosley which, if not startling, at least brought us to the other side of Congleton for lunch.

The sun by this time was shining brightly so that lunch became a pleasantly prolonged affair while we congratulated ourselves on having found fine weather at last. The day we had started was the first fine day near Manchester for almost a month. It had been gloriously sunny yesterday and here was today bright and warm. It seemed we were in luck.

The canal here is becoming densely overgrown with weeds. These make it impassable for motor boats and even the *Hebe* had to be assisted with her oars, the wind not being enough to force a passage.

We were intending to catch a tug through the Harecastle tunnel at about five o'clock, but when we arrived at Hall Green we learned from a passing canal boat that the next tug to go into the tunnel would do so towards seven o'clock. There was nothing to do but wait for two hours. We had a very leisurely tea and then proceeded to drift round the corner to Hardings Wood where the information about the tug was confirmed. We went up and inspected the tunnel and just then a shower came on. Running back a hundred yards we were soon in the shelter of a nearby railway bridge. The shower was quickly over, so seizing a golden opportunity the Mate went ashore and replenished our larder from a little shop he found round the corner.

Not long after his return the canal boats which were to form the seven o'clock convoy began to foregather in a long line stretching from the tunnel mouth. About a quarter before the hour we heard the grinding of the tug's motors as it neared the tunnel mouth. It had eight barges behind and it was a revelation to see how quickly these heavy boats picked up their horses and got away down the locks towards Middlewich. As soon as they were away the convoy for Stoke began to assemble in close formation. Seven barges were there already, and as for safety's sake we were to come last, we did not join the procession until we saw the ticket collector come along the towpath.

Our presence was naturally causing excitement and speculation, and to say the least advice to us was plentiful. The captain of the end boat, to whom we were tied, was especially loquacious. He was evidently feeling the responsibility of having a cock-boat towing astern through the long tunnel.

LONDON & NORTH EASTERN RAILWAY.

............*Canal*............Dept............*Hall Green*............Station.

USL/50 N.º 58541 ....*August 1*............192 0

Received from............*S. Stoker.*............

on account of the **London and North Eastern Railway Company**   UNDER

the sum of ....Pound   TWO

............*Four*............Shillings and............*Ten*............Pence   POUNDS

............*Pleasure Boat.*............

—:4:10   *M H Reynolds* ....Agent or Collector.

Permit dated 1 August 1930. The price was 4*s* 10*d* (see Plate 6).

The ticket collector was a cheery fellow, full of jokes. He collected our 1/3*d* with a smile and was brimming with hints and tips about going through the tunnel. Next came the captain and crew of the electric tug to examine us more closely and give us the benefit of their advice. The crew was the most intelligent man seen so far. He was first to ask if we had a lamp, and we were able to assure him we had a fine one. It was many years old, it was true; it had even reverted to the use of wax candles after many years' service as an oil lamp. The Commander had been trimming it and now it contained a varied assortment of candles. To be sure it was very efficient, but nevertheless it gave off a most unholy smell of burning paint. At one period in its life it had possessed a cunning bit of apparatus whereby it could be made into red, white or green; now in its advanced years it steadfastly refused to show anything but white.

At length the tug started away with a grinding and a groaning and a hysterical screaming. Slowly each barge, one after another, heaved forward a bit, stopped, and then gathered way. It must have been nearly a minute after the tug started that the movement came down to the *Hebe*, and when the tug was entering the tunnel we were nearly two hundred yards from the entrance. The crew of the tug was standing just in the tunnel mouth to inquire if we were alright as we went in.

'Yes, we're alright,' from the *Hebe*.

'Well,' came the reply, 'if anything goes wrong just show your red light,' and he meant what he said. The Commander and Mate had alarming visions of something going wrong; of themselves struggling in the water and at the same time trying to wave the red light.

The daylight slowly receded from the tunnel mouth. Except for the anaemic glow of our lamp nothing could be seen and the motion of the boat was absolutely imperceptible. It was strange, therefore, to hear the noise of falling water getting louder and louder and, at its loudest, to hear drops come pattering along the boat before smoothly splashing astern.

We had not gone far when conversation started with the bargee immediately ahead. We soon knew how far he had come that day, and how far he intended going. We found none of the boats in this convoy intended to go more than two miles beyond the tunnel, so the bargee was the more astonished to learn that we intended to reach Trentham that night. From the tunnel to Trentham lock is eight miles of black but interesting country. It is one long stretch of potteries, wharves and manufactories. It was our idea, therefore, to get out into open country before turning in for the night.

We emerged from the tunnel towards eight o'clock, and although it might mean losing a few minutes we accepted the offer of the bargee to give us a tow as far as he was going. His horse was already waiting so we hardly slackened speed between casting off from the tug and hitching on to the horse.

At Burslem we were again on our own, and bidding farewell to the boatman we swung on our own sweet way. We made such good progress that in half an hour we were leading the procession and heading into the night.

Darkness was beginning to fall in earnest and still there was no place where we could hope to stop. True, at one place we saw a slag heap that offered shelter, but a tin-pot railway was making a racket nearby so we gave that a miss. Suddenly, as we swept along in semi-darkness, the countryside was lit up by a soft red glow. On top of a slag heap was a puny engine pushing a truck from which a great lump of fire had been disgorged. The light from this red hot slag turned night into day while the mass stuck there glowing like the sun. Tiny flames burst out here and there, while occasionally a piece would break off and go tumbling to the bottom. And all the time this pillar of fire remained high up in the air transforming the whole district. Tarrying not we sped on our triumphant way, right through the middle of blast furnaces and ironworks whose gnome-like fiends stared at us in astonishment.

By nine o'clock we had done over five miles in the hour and here was the top lock at Stoke on Trent. There was only sufficient light to see with difficulty and still we were four miles from Trentham. As we went through the lock the last glimmerings of light went out and we were left in darkness.

With the darkness came rain and now we were in a quandary. Fortunately a good bridge offered shelter for the moment, and there, with a dozen helpers to hold us safe, we debated the matter. The rain had settled in well for the night. Trentham and open country was only four miles away. We were in the middle of Stoke, and to cap it all it was pitch dark. A fine situation.

After considering the clouds and the rain the first thing to do was to put up the cover and then everything in the boat would at least be dry. With the cover up the Commander went to spy out the land. The next lock was but a hundred yards away, and just below it a small backwater presented itself. A boat was moored in the entrance but this could easily be circumnavigated.

Accordingly a towrope was fixed, we dropped down the lock, and with a little difficulty gained the shelter of our dock. Half a dozen natives made their appearance and gave us copious advice. We had, it seemed, tied up under the spillway of the lock and would be in danger of swamping if a boat came down. On this information we shifted the *Hebe* about ten yards further on and very soon, in the shelter of the cover, were making hot Bovril. A distant clock chimed the hour and to our surprise it was a quarter after ten.

You may wonder why on a holiday we were so keen to get on. For instance, on the day just recorded we had come nearly twenty miles, through sixteen locks and a long tunnel – a very good performance. The truth was that the next day, Saturday, inaugurated the Stoke Wakes and on Sunday night the canal was due to be stopped and in many places emptied for repair purposes. Naturally we did not want to be caught and so we were pushing along in order to be past Fradley Junction before Monday morning.

SATURDAY 2ND AUGUST

The weather being doubtful we breakfasted on board with the cover over our heads in readiness for the shower which threatened us. The dark clouds passed away without raining on us, so having finished our bacon and eggs and licked up the last spot of marmalade we stowed the cover and its irons and left our sheltering dock.

We had gone less than half a mile when a boatman on the towpath overtook us and cheerfully (or expectantly) shouted that he was going our way and would help us with the locks if we lent him a windlass. Accordingly we enlisted his aid as five locks came close together just here. While waiting under an overhanging roof to avoid a little shower we watched as an upcoming barge got jammed under a beam on the lock gates. This was fortunate from our point of view, as by the time the barge had unjammed itself the rain had stopped and we could carry on in the dry.

It was nearly 11 a.m. by the time we reached Stoke and got away after laying in stores for the weekend. The wind, which was blowing away the clouds so well, had increased to gale force, making towing a necessity. Luckily there were few boats moored to the side so we had little difficulty in keeping the towrope clear. However, when we reached open country the wind was blowing a hurricane and making progress hard. It was so strong that even the barges were being blown about by it. We had to take to the oars and row round the outside of these heavy boats because the wind kept them scraping along the towpath side totally out of control.

The sun came out full and strong after a little while, and though the wind was still lashing the water into waves the going was very pleasant, especially near Trentham where in a rocky gorge we were shielded from the blast. At Trentham we again met lovely country, though the wind was still half a gale, and judging it to be about dinner time we found the lee of a great hedge and settled down to a well-earned meal.

As we were packing up a weird and most memorable apparition approached along the middle of the canal. In general this thing had the appearance of a motor boat. The hull was undeniably that of a motor boat, and withal it had quite handsome lines. It was the superstructure which was puzzling. Forward, a glass-panelled cabin was built, stretching perhaps over a quarter of the boat's length. Ten feet behind this was another similar cabin, and between the two was a sort of canvas covering joining them to make a kind of weather-proof passage.

From the aftermost cabin and stretching over the stern was an awning of green canvas and iron rods.[1] The most curious thing was the wheel situated amidships, so that the steerer had to stand up with his head and shoulders sticking out of the canvas after the manner of a submarine.

We let it pass, and then casting off we started away once more. The wind was still very strong but already beginning to lose some of its force. The sun was doing his best and the day became delightful. Towards five o'clock we reached the locks at Stone. There are eight of them altogether and at the second we overtook the motor boat affair which had passed us at dinner time. Her crew were scattered about and as far as we could judge seemed to consist of:

- The Captain, a man of about 50
- His wife
- Their numerous progeny all dressed in blue dungarees
- A nurse
- A mechanic

We went down the lock before them, having the help of the second daughter and the two younger boys. By the time we reached number eight the inner man was complaining and we sought a quiet nook beneath some trees and soon had the kettle singing on the stove.

The wind which had been so strong against us during the day was now, by a lucky turn in the canal, in our favour. So when tea was over we hastened to break out all sail, but in the aggravating way the wind has it incontinently dropped to the merest zephyr and we settled down to drifting. We soon had again to turn to the oars, and finally by bedtime had reached the neighbourhood of Weston, sixteen miles from Etruria, our morning's starting place.

---

1. I don't know if this had a later bearing on him, but oddly enough when he had his first two narrowboats converted he had cabins fore and aft and an open deck between them. The two were joined by an overhead plank and a canvas could be stretched over it for extra cover. As both were butties, steering was always from the traditional place. Certainly the central well was excellent for al fresco meals and extra accommodation.

SUNDAY 3RD AUGUST

There was no sign of yesterday's tempestuous weather when we awoke, and the sun was shining brightly. The air was so warm and the water so clear and inviting that we seized the opportunity to bathe before breakfast, so creating a wonderful appetite which was made even more keen by the smell of bacon sizzling in the pan and the aroma of coffee scenting the air.

Two village rustics came up the opposite bank as we put the last touches to our breakfast, and from then until we moved off they stood there, mouths busy catching flies and eyes bulging as if they were petrified at the sight of us. As far as we could judge – for we had no watch – it was about 10.30 when we at last bid farewell to our rustics and rowed away in perfect weather.

From here to Great Haywood the locks are fairly frequent, although they do not occur so often as to be a nuisance. Great Haywood itself, a charmingly situated village, is – or was – an important canal junction. Here the northern end of the Staffordshire and Worcestershire Canal meets the great traffic route between the Trent and the Mersey. In the course of time, and after wandering around Birmingham, the *Hebe* would join the Staffs and Worcs midway on its length.

When we arrived at Great Haywood lock there was a slight contretemps. Where was the Commander's windlass? It was not in the bows, nor yet in the stern. It could not be found under the sail and was not under the floorboards. The Commander had used it a mile back at the last lock, so we concluded it must have been left there, and while he went back to look for it the Mate locked the *Hebe* through. The windlass was an important part of our equipment, for without it the passage of some locks would be impossible. So in spite of the distance to the last lock, and in spite of the hot sun, off went the Commander for his little instrument.

He had not gone far when he met with a stroke of good fortune. A canal boat coming through the lock in our wake had seen the windlass and picked it up. They knew it belonged to someone ahead of them and that someone would be coming back for it. The Commander was naturally as delighted to regain it as the boatman was to have been able to be of service. Then, running on ahead, the Commander saw the *Hebe* was through the lock and made it ready for the barge.

Once through the lock we moored in the shade of the great wood through which hereabouts the canal runs and proceeded to dinner. It was a memorable meal in many respects. The Commander had, while foraging in Stoke, bought an enormous beefsteak and this was very quickly sizzling in the pan. It was, we fear, no steak from the youngest and tenderest calf, but rather a slice from some fierce old bull. By dint of pounding it and frying until our patience was exhausted we succeeded in rendering it very palatable and fell to with great gusto.

The country around was picturesque. On one side of the canal was a wood of huge beeches and on the other was the clearing of Shugborough Hall. The Hall itself stood at the other side of the clearing round which the woods closed in on every side. The River Sow wound in and out, sparkling in the sunlight, so that we almost forsook the canal for the river. Through the whole landscape only ourselves and the occasional bird or rabbit moved, a Sunday hush pervaded everything so that even the sunbeams seemed to shine more softly than on other days, and the trees were as though drawn on canvas.

We were now on a nine-mile pound, and at Rugeley a tall chapel is to be seen amongst a thick grove of trees. This is a monastery where can be seen white-robed monks going about feeding hens, sowing seed and even hanging out the washing. The place is as silent as the grave. So quiet, indeed, it might be a fairy tale.

At Colwich the canal runs past the village green where, when we went by, thirty men were throwing dice while the village idiot hung round the outskirts of the crowd in a state of some considerable *négligé*. On sighting us the same fellow collected himself as best he could and ran along after us bending double and straightening up in a pretended style of rowing, all the while his clothes falling off. He was shouting: 'Yer b—— fools yer'll be out of breath.' A few yards took us out of sight of this simpleton and into quiet country again.

After tea we set out for Fradley through charming country. We had made a slight mistake in reading our map and imagining we still had nine miles to go we put on a bit of a spurt. Imagine our surprise, therefore, when we came upon the next lock at about nine p.m. we learned that Fradley was close at hand, not more than a mile distant, and that a little over twenty minutes would bring us to the turning just below the fourth lock. Between the second and third locks we were astonished to find people holidaying on the canal. It was a troop of scouts who had chartered a canal boat and horse and were living on board under the tarpaulins usually used to protect the cargo.

At Fradley the swing bridge across the entrance to the Coventry Canal was locked up with an enormous padlock, dating, we judged, from the Norman Conquest. A little persuasion, however, soon unfastened the bridge and we gently paddled through into a fearfully dark and still canal. So rigid were the reflections on the water that one might have thought it impossible to be fluid at all.

We went on and on looking for a convenient camping spot without success, until finally we gave up and tied to a high bank with a potato field at the top.

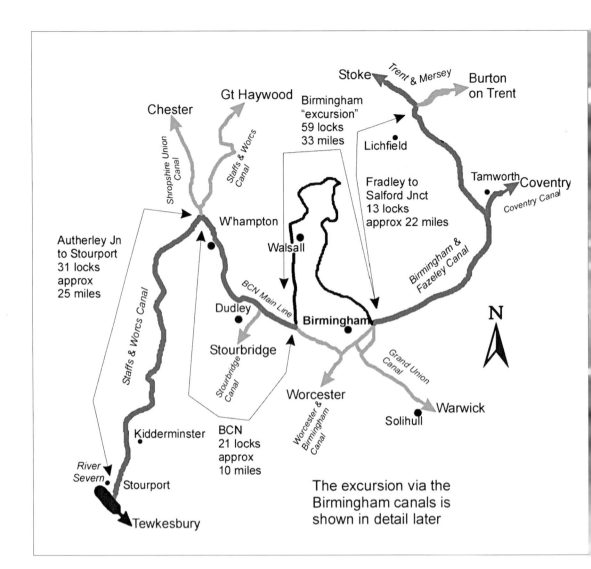

Stoke
Trent & Mersey
Burton on Trent
Gt Haywood
Birmingham "excursion" 59 locks 33 miles
Chester
Lichfield
Shropshire Union Canal
Staffs & Worcs Canal
Fradley to Salford Jnct 13 locks approx 22 miles
Tamworth Coventry
Coventry Canal
W'hampton
Autherley Jn to Stourport 31 locks approx 25 miles
Walsall
Birmingham & Fazeley Canal
Staffs & Worcs Canal
BCN Main Line
Dudley
Birmingham
N
Stourbridge
Grand Union Canal
Stourbridge Canal
Worcester
Warwick
River Severn
Kidderminster
BCN 21 locks approx 10 miles
Worcester & Birmingham Canal
Solihull
Stourport
The excursion via the Birmingham canals is shown in detail later
Tewkesbury

Fradley to Stourport.

Chapter II

The Birmingham Canals

MONDAY 4TH AUGUST

In the morning were were awakened early by the noise of raindrops on the cover. Having now no need to hurry past any particular point we were not at all perturbed.

During breakfast we heard a horse coming along the towpath and looked out to behold the Scouts' boat going by. The horse, its driver, and the two steerers could not have looked wetter if they had just come out of the canal. With great alarm we noticed the boat swinging about the canal and the two small boys at the helm having a great argument as to which way to put the tiller. We heaved a sigh of relief when this juggernaut went safely by, pounding and scraping the opposite bank.

About two hours after this the rain abated and we set out. The wind was in our favour and 'reaching gale force at times'. Consequently when we broke out our mainsail we soon went bowling along at great speed, especially past Huddlesford[1] where the rustic fauna in large quantities stood and gaped in amazement.

We were sweeping along so well that the two-hour lead gained by the Scouts' boat steadily decreased, even though they were travelling light. The distance they were ahead could be judged by asking the fishermen how long it was since the Scouts went by. At Huddlesford Junction we were over an hour and a quarter behind them, so we crowded on all sail and slowly drew nearer and nearer. In spite of a stop for provisions near Whittington Brook when we plunged into the immense Hopwas Wood we were only half an hour behind.

---

1. Huddlesford Junction with the Wyrley and Essington Canal.

The turreted bridge. This picture was taken on a later trip in 1974 (see Plate 8).

Still faster and faster we sailed, curling the water under the lee and making it go racing past in a fury of bubbles. At one point we took shelter under a bridge until a shower blew over, and then on we went with everything taut and quivering.

In the early afternoon we approached Fazeley, the junction for Birmingham. There was some satisfaction because instead of being two hours ahead the scouts were only ten minutes away. We were not, it appeared, destined to overtake the scouts as they carried on to Coventry while we made for Birmingham.

At Fazeley we turned though an angle of more than ninety degrees so naturally we lost the advantages of the wind and had to resort to the oar. Almost immediately we passed under Watling Street, teeming with traffic and half hidden in a cloud of dust.

Many of the canal bridges hereabouts are, we felt sure, due to flights of imagination on the part of the architect. One in particular fascinated us. To be sure it was only a footbridge, but what a wonderful structure. At each side of the canal was a battlemented turret, cylindrical in shape and about thirty feet high. Between the tops of these towers stretched a narrow wooden gangway and access to the bridge was gained through the turrets up a winding staircase. It gave the impression that the canal was passing through some ancient keep. The country is very pretty round here but is rapidly being spoilt by the construction of great numbers of red–brick, blue–slate, dog kennels they nowadays call houses.

In the early evening we drifted on and reached Curdworth. Here the bottom lock was closed for the Bank Holiday. The crowd of natives gathered there were naturally full of advice and help. What were we to do? It was still some hours until dusk, and at all events we did not want to have to turn back. The general consensus was that we could get through [the locks] that night if we found the lock keeper who had the key. All very well, but where was this important official? He had been out on an excursion but, we were told, he would certainly be back by now. In any case the key would be at his house.

'Ah yes,' said the Commander, 'where does he live?'

'Well,' said the leader of the chorus, 'his house is the second of the row at the third lock. If you can ride I'll lend you my bike.'

The Commander being a more or less accomplished rider accepted the offer, and leaping into the saddle rode away in search of the elusive lockman. At the house the Commander learned he would probably be at the sixth lock, but when he got there he found an old man digging potatoes who strenuously denied that he was the lock keeper.

'No I'm not the lock keeper. He's further up the canal. What d'ye want him for? Ye canna get through tonight. He winna let ye, besides it'll be dark long before ye reach the top.'

Not stopping to hear the rest of this peroration, for obviously the old pessimist had only just started, the Commander raced away up the towpath in search of this phantom being. Nearing the two mile mark he found the towpath obstructed by half a dozen people, and calling in a loud voice quickly discovered his man.

A little persuasion was necessary. The Commander pointed out we were strangers in a strange land. Not only that but we were in an open boat and it was imperative to go on. He ended on a strong note hinting at murder and death. This convinced our friend and he came out with, 'Well, per'aps I might let you through like, here's the key. Go on down to the bottom lock and I'll foller ye.'

With the all-important key in his pocket the Commander made haste to rejoin the *Hebe*. Returning the cycle with due thanks to its owner he unloosed the padlock and up we went. At the second lock we met the lock keeper who, having procured a cycle, proposed to accompany us through the remaining locks.

Typical narrow lock.
From an original glass
negative.

At number ten, however, this friend left us and we ran for the shelter of a bridge to get out of the rain which was beginning to fall. It was now about nine o'clock, so not waiting for the shower to blow over, which it did within ten minutes, we put up the cover and, finding a convenient bank, moored for the night.

TUESDAY 5TH AUGUST

We were awakened early by the sound of a lorry passing over a nearby bridge, and on rising found the sun blazing from a cloudless sky. Naturally, therefore, we were soon away and taking advantage of the little airs that were playing along the canal.

The Birmingham canals are notable for long straight stretches. In places these reaches are bordered with brick for miles. It certainly keeps the towpath in good order but from the beauty point of view they leave a lot to be desired. The lockage is fairly heavy but there were few places where the locks were really close together.

As we approached Castle Bromwich we became increasingly aware of an aerodrome. Never five minutes passed but a plane would circle and land. We were beginning to wonder at this great number of aeroplanes when we happened to note a registration mark. Lo and behold! In less than twenty minutes that same aeroplane flew over twice. In a little while we came nearer and our suspicions were confirmed. There were but three or four machines in all but they were making very frequent flights and we smiled at their stupidity. How could the crew of such a famous ship be gulled by such a stratagem? Not only that but how could they hope to deceive the Mate, a descendant of the very people who had won the battle of Pllowytrocogog!

By and by we sailed past the important Salford Junction. Three canals, the Warwick and Birmingham,[2] the Birmingham and Fazeley, and the Tame Valley all meet at this point in one great pool.

To guard the entrance to these canals is an important row of toll collectors' offices. The *Hebe* sliding gently by went past without so much as disturbing one toll keeper from his siesta. Soon after this we came to the bottom of the flight of locks at Perry Bar.[3] Deciding that before ascending this great staircase it would be better to feed, we tied up to the bank and made lunch.

As we were just finishing we observed a young man, hatless and without a coat, tearing along the canal behind us at a really dangerous speed. The news of our presence had at last filtered through to a toll keeper and this was the result. Giving him time to regain his breath and cool down at little we finished our lunch and punted across the canal to allow him to examine our credentials. This done we ascended the thirteen locks at Perry Bar.

We were now within easy distance of the centre of Birmingham. Feeling that we must at all costs see the city, we left the *Hebe* in the care of a lock keeper who tied her with padlock and chain to an enormous barge.

Setting off, we soon found a convenient omnibus and boarded it as both the driver and conductor promised it would take us into the city. It was a nice bus but its progress, when once started, was distinctly spasmodic. Perhaps it objected to the two hooligans seated on top. Finally as it was passing its stables it stopped altogether, and when the driver had spoken with the authorities we were all bundled out and into a monstrous relic of the last century.

---

2. This was incorporated into the Grand Union Canal.
3. On the Tame Valley Canal. There are thirteen locks altogether, the lower ones being now under Spaghetti Junction.

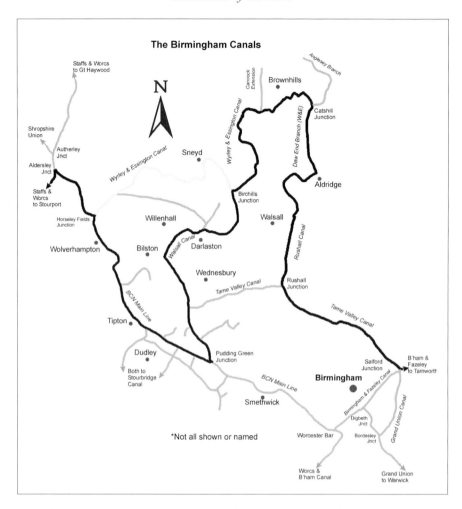

The Birmingham Canals

My father was always more interested in the country around than the construction of the canals he was on. This makes his narrative of the Birmingham area especially difficult to trace. However, I have pieced together a best guess of the route, taking into account the landmarks he *has* bothered to mention and the fact that to have seen the Ocker Hill engine he must have been in the Tipton area. This would mean that he would have come along the Walsall Canal. As far as I can judge the route was thus:

Salford Junction to Rushall Junction	13 locks	5 miles
Rushall Branch to Daw End Branch	9 locks	3 miles
Daw End Branch (of Wyrley & Essington)	0 locks	7 miles
Walsall Canal (Birchills – Pudding Green)	16 locks	8 miles
(inc. Wednesbury Old Canal link)		
BCN Main Line to Aldersley Junction	21 locks	10 miles
Total	59 locks	33 miles

(If this is not correct then no doubt someone will say so!)

After a long – and – roundabout – journey we eventually arrived in the city, where the Commander now proposed to show the Mate around. Following a short sightseeing tour he led the way to a gilded eating house where we were taken for peers of the realm. The owners argued 'who but the highest in the land would have the brass neck to enter a high class establishment such as this in that attire. Mary this way. James attend that table. Ah yes sir, what would you like?'[4]

The best of things come to an end and at last we had to leave this regal atmosphere. There were a few things still to be done, and when these were completed we bent our steps again to the *Hebe*. She was safe and sound, so thanking the lock keeper for all his care we started off along the Tame Valley. When the time arrived we could not decide on a camping site. Just when we should have stopped for the night we came to a great long straight stretch with tall banks on each side and which offered no harbourage. It usually turns out thus when it comes to stopping for the night. Each day we say: 'Well, we'll be sure to stop in good time tonight.' Then in the evening: 'There's a nice place,' from someone. 'No, no,' from someone else, 'I do not like the shape of that tree, might fall down y'know, let's go on a little.' And so that place is too high, this one too low, the other is not sheltered enough, and over there are too many animals. As time goes by one place after another is vetoed until finally we are forced to camp anywhere, and discover in the morning we are right on someone's doorstep or just under a stone chute.

This night, however, was an exception to the rule for we could still see each other before turning in. A good site was found on the Rushall Branch which turned off the main line just before we came to the end of the cutting.

WEDNESDAY 6TH AUGUST

This day was not particularly noteworthy in any respect. The weather was grey and uninspiring and the country uninteresting. Here and there we managed to put in a little sailing but the wind, such as it was, was for the most part adverse.

At Catshill Junction we were held up at the stop while a barge load of coal was measured, and as we set off again a crowd of urchins and local unemployed on cycles sallied forth and accompanied us for a mile or so. During the course

---

4. I well remember ADS using just such inverted snobbery at the Tontine in Stourport, which he entered in his habitual blue boiler suit! Mine host decided only a VIP would have the gall to do so.

Wolverhampton, from a contemporary postcard.

of the afternoon we skirted a colliery at Ocker Hill. To our amazement we saw one of James Watt's beam engines still working. Pieces of similar beam engines can be seen in museums where they are regarded as great curios.[5]

By the evening we were approaching the precincts of Wolverhampton, and not wishing to pass that town at night we tied up near a disused bridge which rejoiced in the name of Devil's Elbow. Two minutes after we got the cover up the rain came pattering down, but that was not enough to drive away the crowd of curious schoolgirls who stood on the opposite bank making remarks both personal and general and every now and then bursting into song.

---

5. This was almost certainly the engine built in 1784 to re-circulate water from the Walsall Canal via a short branch. It closed only in 1948 but remained intact until 1960. The site was not far from Boulton & Watt's original Soho Foundry works. In his later years my father was heavily involved with the restoration of the Cromford Canal, which included the restoration of the great Cornish-type beam engine at Leawood, built to pump water into that canal.

Chapter III

Down to the River Severn

THURSDAY 7TH AUGUST

That morning we awoke in the best of spirits knowing we should soon be on the delightful Staffordshire and Worcestershire Canal. While we were putting the last touches to packing the boat a barge was approaching which, on drawing level, offered us a tow. Acting on the impulse of a moment we threw him a rope and were slowly drawn along in the barge's wake.

Towards twelve o'clock we found ourselves right in the middle of Wolverhampton, and casting off from the barge which was going Bilston way, we were soon at the top of the flight of twenty-one locks leading down to Tettenhall. At this point we found a knot of interested spectators, bargees for the most part, all full of hints and warnings as to our conduct through the locks.

Twenty-one locks is a good step, so when two juvenile boatmen who knew the canal offered their services in helping us down the locks we gladly accepted their tender. It is the rule here that, when going down, water must not be run out of an upper lock until the water is being let into the lock below. In accordance with this the Mate went on ahead to prepare each lock for the *Hebe*.

As it was necessary for the *Hebe* party to refrain from emptying a lock until the Mate was drawing paddles below, so it was necessary for those with the *Hebe* to be able to see him. The canal, of course, is not straight and usually a lower lock can only be seen by an expert on the upper. Where a stranger cannot see down the canal, a knowing pilot can save his legs considerably. Experience shows that in most cases the next lock can just be seen from some particular point, and this is where our helpers were so useful. One of them was cognisant of all the view points. Thus at one lock he would lie on his face and peer under the beams, at another he would be on top of the boundary fence. Only once did he have to go and look round a corner to see if the Mate was ready.

We put the last of the locks behind us at about one o'clock, and bidding farewell to our companions slid away on the Stafford and Worcester Canal. We did not go far before choosing a quiet spot out of the sun and under the trees which border the race course where we stopped for a hearty lunch. We were now in the neighbourhood of Tettenhall where, strangely, quite a lively interest is taken in pleasure boating.

One of these boats took our fancy in particular, on account of its wonderful rudder lines. They were made of rope nearly two inches in diameter. The old lady steering could not get her hand right round them. They certainly added an air of distinction to the boat, for they were scrubbed white as snow.

Tettenhall was a place at which correspondence was to be collected. The Mate, because he had not seen the town before, went off in search of the letters at the Post Office. The Gods had indeed been good, for waiting at the Post Office was an enormous parcel full of good things to eat. The Mate returned as fast as he could to the *Hebe* and we spent an exciting half hour in exploration.

A circular weir similar to the ones described below. This picture was taken on a later trip in 1971 (see Plate 9).

The boat was now so loaded that when we hoisted sail we naturally did not progress at an astonishing pace. Nevertheless, we passed the Compton Queen and were below Compton Lock before teatime.

The canal here meanders through beautiful pastoral country. All the time we were following the valley of the Stour, and falling with it to the level of the Severn at Stourport. The fields were luxuriantly green, dotted with wonderful trees and bounded by flowering hedgerows. Vegetation approaches the sub-tropical. A real tree in this part of the country will shelter half an army under its branches. The locks are charming pieces of work which merge into the scenery so well as to appear almost natural. They are all equipped with a sort of giant's hand basin on one side. In fact they are exactly like big basins. The water wells up darkly all around the brim, overlaps it and goes rushing down the inside in a white cascade to disappear down a hole in the centre.

We wandered on all day through this Arcady until the fading light made us draw in for the night in the shelter of a willow grove near Dimingsdale. The moon on these nights was drawing to its full quarter and on this night, with no cloud, we saw a harvest moon in all its glory. It appeared over the crest of a hill, standing stationary when looked at but mounting the sky with incredible speed when one's back was turned. It seemed about twenty times its normal size, and so near we thought a hand might almost touch it.[1] A yellow orb, it was an unforgettable sight, so much so that we felt our time would not be wasted were we to turn back now.

FRIDAY 9TH AUGUST

The day came with bright sun sparkling on the dewdrops and we hurried to get started. In the same subtle way that salmon sense the sea, so was the *Hebe* feeling the proximity of the river. The wind was blowing Severnwards, so hoisting sail we were soon speeding along to the Bratch.

The Bratch is a collection of three locks very close together and making a drop in the canal of about seventy feet. There are two ways of working these locks. If one way is attempted the countryside may be flooded when the water rises above the level of the lower locks. The other way, although meaning more work, allows excess water to pour down a sluice.

Naturally the Commander took the line of least resistance and, as the surrounding country was under the greatest depth of water, the lock keeper

---

1. Not surprising. The full moon that month was the next day, 9 August.

The Bratch Locks (Nos 23–25) from an original glass negative. These three locks are often referred to as a staircase, but in fact they are not. The original canal, planned by Brindley, opened in 1772 and did indeed have a three-lock staircase, but they were later re-engineered as three individual locks, albeit separated by incredibly short pounds of only a few feet (as can be seen in this picture). That is why it is so easy, when emptying an upper lock, to flood 'the surrounding country' as the water is likely to overtop the spillways and the upper gates of the next lock. Care and common sense is always required on such structures.

Kinver, from a contemporary postcard (see Plate 10).

put in an appearance, wading up the steps to the lock down which a cascade was pouring. Fortunately he was in a genial frame of mind and made no particular objection, going so far only as to demonstrate the correct method.

As we went through the second lock, a young fellow with a windlass in hand appeared on the bank. He was obviously not a bargee so we were both anxious for a glimpse of his craft. Leaving the bottom lock we saw a Canadian canoe blessed – or cursed – with the name *St Swithin*. It had left Worcester several days before and was bound for Shrewsbury and the upper waters of the Severn.

The pilot in charge of this frail craft was, like his companion, dressed in clothes unlikely to be harmed by any sudden immersion in the canal. Such immersion seemed imminent, the canoe being loaded down to within a very few inches of the water.

At Kinver we almost took tea in a quiet garden but a little further on a pleasant bank invited, which we found most suitable. Unfortunately, it appeared also to be a favourite spot with the village belles, who were continually passing by smirking and sniggering.

The day had been furiously hot and we had taken things easily, but now in the cool of the evening we were in great form, especially as there was just a chance of reaching the Severn that night.

At Cookley Lock, as we were about to go down, a barge came up behind us. Naturally, being the only pleasure craft, we gave way and they drew into the lock before us. Chatting with the bargee, he ridiculed our suggestion that we might be in Stourport before nightfall.

'Get to Stour tonight, that ye won't. Even we won't get to Stour by then.'

We did not like this disparagement of the *Hebe* and pointed out we could go a good deal faster than a barge.

'What?', from the boatman. 'We'll be a lock ahead of you and you can't make that up.'

This we took as a challenge, and finding that the next lock was two miles ahead we swore the *Hebe* would be the first there.

The barge then drew out of the lock, and so started quite an epic race. Remember it was only two miles to the next lock, and the lock we were at had to be filled and emptied again before we could start forward. By the time the *Hebe* was ready to slide out of the lock that barge was eight minutes ahead and well out of sight. However, we took short sharp spells at the oars, our prow fairly cutting through the water. So fast did we go that in a mile we were only a biscuit's toss away from our rival. Fetching out the towrope we passed him and continued on our triumphal way, promising to leave the lock ready for him.

By eight o'clock we were passing the carpet mills of Kidderminster. We were to call for letters there, but at this time of night the Post Office would be shut, so we decided to carry on to Stourport and take the 'bus into Kidderminster the next morning – a perfectly feasible scheme according to the fishermen we consulted.

Hurrying on, we were within easy reach of Stourport by about a quarter past nine. It was thought best not to get onto the Severn so late, not only because of the difficulty of camping on the river near there but also because there was some doubt about the lock into the river being open after eight.

Eventually we came to a wide pool in the canal, sheltered on two sides by a sandstone cliff and on another by a deep wood. Here, under the wide spreading branches of a Spanish chestnut tree, we slept the sleep of the just.

Chapter IV

Stourport to Evesham

SATURDAY 9TH AUGUST

On Saturday morning the weather was rather dull but we got away as near as we could judge about ten o'clock, or perhaps a little earlier, we did not know.

Just as we were pushing off, who should come up from Stourport but our friend of the night before. By rising at four o'clock, he had gone down to Stourport and unloaded, and here he was coming back. Although technically he had beaten us to the actual wharf, he was very astonished at the distance we had made before stopping. So astonished was he, that he made haste to spread the news of our feat and on our return journey we found ourselves with a great reputation for speed.

A mile and a half and we found ourselves at a lock leading into a great basin. Here were many signs of decayed canal traffic. There were two enormous docks surrounded by warehouses for all kinds of commodities, and all the business going on was a little coal being unloaded. Except for a few senile pleasure boats, this once busy centre of commerce was deserted. In the heyday of its existence these docks had been so busy that separate incoming and outgoing locks had been built.

Here we beheld one of the most curious-looking boats it has ever been our lot to inspect. We were familiar with electric tramcars and also with barges, but here was a cross between the two. A wonderful craft. We do not attempt to explain it; the fact just stands that here was an actual cross between a canal boat and a tramcar.

Down the next lock and then came the glorious sensation of slowly gliding out of the high walls of a seven-foot lock onto the broad waters of the River Severn. Here is a noble river and well thought of by the dwellers

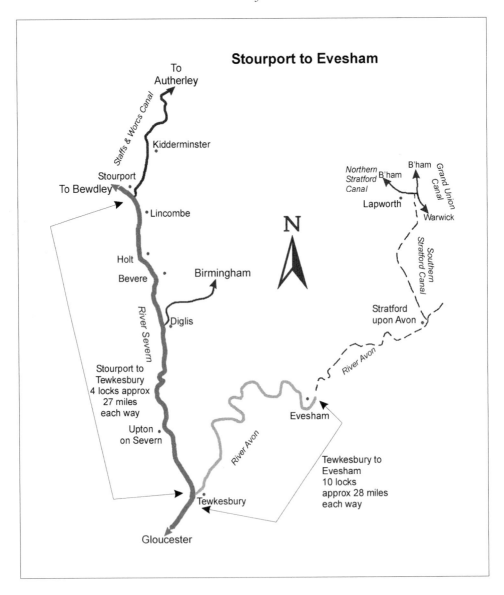

Stourport to Evesham

To Autherley

Staffs & Worcs Canal

Kidderminster

Stourport

To Bewdley

Lincombe

Holt

Bevere

Birmingham

N

River Severn

Diglis

Northern Stratford Canal

B'ham

B'ham

Grand Union Canal

Lapworth

Warwick

Southern Stratford Canal

Stratford upon Avon

Stourport to
Tewkesbury
4 locks approx
27 miles
each way

River Avon

Upton on Severn

Evesham

River Avon

Tewkesbury to
Evesham
10 locks
approx 28 miles
each way

Tewkesbury

Gloucester

on its banks. Unlike so many other of our English streams, Sabrina does not flow neglected but bears some very fine craft on her bosom.

Turning upstream we headed the *Hebe* for a floating landing stage. While we were yet fifty yards off, a boatman was ready, clearing the stage and preparing for us with fender and boathook. This courtesy won our hearts completely, and leaving the *Hebe* under his charge we set off in search of a Kidderminster 'bus.

The town was crowded with visitors and we had to stand in the 'bus all the way to Kidderminster. Here, after some little delay in finding the Post Office,

The Severn at Stourport.

we collected letters which had been following us all round the country since we started.

There is very little to note in Kidderminster. It is a typical English market town, round which the carpet industry has sprung up. The town is also credited with the fact that it was the birthplace of Rowland Hill, responsible for the introduction of penny postage.

When we returned to our 'bus we were just in time to see it disappear round the corner. Picking up our heels we tore through narrow twisty streets after the vehicle, and in the course of time when we had run nearly half a mile we succeeded in catching the eye of the conductor who stopped the 'bus for us, and in a short time we were back in Stourport.

Leaving the 'bus at the top of the main street we slowly made our way down to the river, collecting eggs at this shop, bread at that, vegetables over the way, until by the time we regained the *Hebe* we were overloaded by parcels and bundles.

Casting off from the landing stage below the bridge, we were smoothly and rapidly borne away on the current. It was a new sensation to us who had been used to the canal for so long.

Downstream we went, past the lovely households and spruce yachts, past the confluence of the Stour, past the big electricity works to Lincomb Lock.

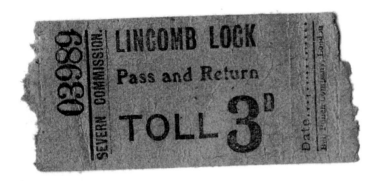

Ticket for the
Lincomb Lock (see
Plate 11).

The sun was now shining out of a cloudless sky, so our first impression of the Severn was very favourable.

We did not go down the lock immediately but moored under the sandstone cliffs, for which Stourport is famed, and cooked our dinner.

When we had emerged from Lincomb Lock and were again on the mainstream, we made a great pretence of sailing. At first there was a very slight breeze and we sailed in great style past pretty bungalows dotted along the banks. Later, however, the zephyr failed us altogether. It was too hot to make any attempt at rowing, so we lolled in the stern sheets (there was no other craft in sight) and slipped downstream on the current, making remarkably good progress. In this fashion we crept down past Hampstall and Holt locks, till we got above Bevere lock. Here, choosing a deep corner of the stream, we had a glorious swim followed by a delightful tea.

Towards half past six when we again started, the evening was ridiculously pleasant. Feeling in fine fettle we straightened our backs and *Hebe* was soon sliding into Worcester. We intended to look round the city but when we saw the crowds in the streets and guessed what it must be like off the water we decided to carry on and forego our visit.

At Diglis lock we only got through after a little difficulty. We shouted ourselves hoarse, but eventually had to go ashore and wake up the lock keeper. Having gained the lower level we were slipping silently past the willows when we were treated to a wonderful sight. All was quiet and still; there was not enough wind to absorb the gentle mist on the surface of the water when suddenly, out of the depths, shot a salmon. Up and up into the air he went, clearing the water by a good twelve feet, then turning over he fell back with a great splash. This is a wonderful enough sight at a waterfall where everything is moving and all nature seems active, but here in the dead stillness of a summer evening the feat was something short of miraculous, with not a little of the uncanny in it.

Camped on the River Teme, from an original glass negative.

On the lookout for a safe mooring place for the night we found the River Teme. Going up it for a little way and skilfully navigating fallen trees, we found a lovely site under an old willow, round whose gnarled roots the waters were lapping and gurgling some age-old tune.

SUNDAY 10TH AUGUST

The lovely bells of Worcester Cathedral ringing out Tom Bowling served to waken us and soon we were splashing in the crystal stream.

The sun was striking the water in golden flecks as it filtered through the leaves. A deep quiet pervaded everything, except for the river, which as it swept along ever and anon gave a happy gurgle among the roots, while the bells lent an added harmony of sound to those of colour and scent.

In the idyllic frame of mind associated with such surrounding we progressed gently downstream. An unfavourable wind impeded us slightly but, by holding under the bank, we were sheltered from it to a great extent, and yet still had the advantage of the current.

Towards midday a few spots of rain threatened to become a heavy shower so, finding some overhanging willows, we took shelter. The shower did not materialise but a monstrous blustering motor launch did. Lashing its way

Worcester Cathedral, from the original glass negative.

downstream it didn't give any consideration at all for other craft. We pushed out from the bank as fast as we could, but nevertheless so great was the wash that the rebounding waves came splashing in over the gunwhale. Fortunately all our important things were under cover, so the water got down to the well without doing much damage. However, it was a boorish display of lack of courtesy on their part. It is at such times that one wishes to be in command of a good quality torpedo boat.

Lock stream on the Severn.

The Severn at Upton, from a contemporary postcard (see Plate 12).

LOWER AVON NAVIGATION.

No. 739

............................**19**.....

Issued by..

Collector at Avon Lock. Tewkesbury.

Name or No. of Vessel.	Owner,	Steerer.
Hebe	Stoker	

From............................ To............................

T.	C.	Q.	Wey.		@	£	s.	d.
			1	Rowing Boat Return			1	6
				LOCKAGE				
					£		1	6

Received by .... *Collector.*

Left: Permit from Lower Avon Navigation, dated 10 August 1930.

Below: Tewkesbury Abbey.

150

King John's Bridge.

Although the morning had been a typical bit of grey Severn day, yet the afternoon was very pleasant. The breeze had lost all its strength while the sun made a gallant effort to shine. We had tea in a wide bend of the river where the banks were so high that we were forced to stay on board the whole time – a motor boat occupied the only available landing ground. Its owner/driver sauntered along the bank afterwards and we opened a very interesting conversation – the long tales of the Commander seemed particularly to intrigue him. He was very sceptical about the *Hebe*'s chances of reaching Evesham.

'Oh no!' he said, 'the locks are broken and the channel is all silted up. The navigation is done for, we never try to go up there.'

We pointed out that the *Hebe* was wont to go where no motor boat would dare to follow, and that we considered a haunt of motor boats no place for a refined craft like her. In spite of this we parted good friends, he to Worcester and we to Tewkesbury.

Upton-on-Severn was passed in great style and then a lookout for Tewkesbury and the Avon was kept. It seemed as though Tewkesbury was as elusive as the rainbow. At every bend we expected to see the Mythe bridge but continually we would be disappointed. The corner would turn out to be no corner at all and just another long reach would open out ahead. We had almost given up hope when suddenly the graceful span appeared, and beyond it the tower of the Abbey and we knew we were near the confluence of the rivers.

Soon we had got into the stream leading up to the town lock, past a long wharf on which most of the youth of the town seemed to be fishing. The lock keeper was absent when we arrived but, just as the Commander had opened the lower gates to admit the *Hebe*, he appeared with a stump of cigar between his teeth.

Lockage having been duly paid we bade farewell to the keeper (who told us that business was improving: 'Why we get that big grain barge through every week') and shooting King John's Bridge hoisted sail and sped upstream in front of the eyes of a crowd of admiring spectators.[1]

MONDAY 11TH AUGUST

The sun was shining strongly when we arose on Monday morning. We found the Avon a delightful river for swimming. Before setting away upstream we returned to Tewkesbury to replenish our larder, leaving *Hebe* at Bathurst's, whose man was very emphatic about a mooring fee.

By the time the Mate had visited the barber and the Commander the Post Office, when the excellent Mr Alder had filled our store, and the Abbey had been visited, it was approaching midday. It was too hot to hurry back to the *Hebe* for lunch so we fed at the Sign of the Ancient Grudge.

Lunch over, we strolled back to the river to find our boat still safe and sound. A breeze was blowing upstream so we hurried to get away and soon were bearing towards Pershore at a fine pace. Past picturesque Twyning Ferry, round the village of Bredon with its lovely old tithe barn, and on to Strensham.

This country seemed to hold a particular fascination for Westall:

[The] Vale of Evesham is renowned both for its beauty and wonderful fertility, and as the river runs for many miles through this blissful Eden, past the foot of the mighty Bredon Hill and almost under the shadow of the Malverns, the Avon may claim to rank among the fairest of England's picturesque rivers.

---

1. The Lower Avon Navigation was privately owned at that time (Bradshaw quotes *The Trustees of the late Edmund Perrot Esq.*) and measured 28 miles, 2 furlongs, with a total of 9 locks.

Strensham Lock was the scene of a mighty insult. The Commander went ashore, and after much expenditure of energy and strength succeeded in preparing the lock. Just as the gate was getting fully open a self-conceited motorboat party, steered by a rheumaticky old geezer in a Panama hat, came fussing round the corner, failed to take the corner properly, grazed the *Hebe's* lovely varnish, went hard astern and then going ahead went into the lock without so much as a by-your-leave. To crown it all they stuck in the entrance and kept us waiting for ten or fifteen minutes. When, eventually, they did get in, they took the best birth and when the *Hebe* came in showed a tendency to crush her.

In the course of time the upper gate was opened and we had another long wait. The other boat was opposite the opened gate, and being power-driven we naturally expected them to go first. Not a bit of it. In spite of many attempts their engine would not start, so losing patience we drew out and were half a mile away before they came in sight trailing clouds of smoke. To calm our ruffled spirits we landed on the bank and made tea.

The evening was delightful as we again started out, passing Eckington Bridge, and the sun smiled lazily down on us as we came to Nafford. The lock here, although workable, was in a very stiff condition and the combined strength of the crew was necessary to open the gates. There was a houseboat moored above the lock and to the great delectation of the Mate a fair Damsel – the daughter of the houseboat – was sitting at the lock side, sketching or writing or what not. So enchanted was he by this vision that when he took up the rudder lines after the locking operation was over he almost steered us down the weir.

Just below Pershore the stream is very narrow on account of the weeds which grow thick on both sides. The water was swirling and tearing down at a tremendous rate so that when we eventually got above the reeds we had done something to be proud of. There we found to our great delight that the town lock, pronounced impassable at Tewkesbury, was in very good condition.

Above it the river is a beautiful broad reach of water, made even more so on this occasion by the last rays of the setting sun tinging the ripples with fiery red. We gently swung along past the Angel and found a camping place below Wyre lock as the lamps were lit in Pershore.

TUESDAY 12TH AUGUST[2]

The bells of Pershore Abbey told us the time as we started next morning. We recollected with amazement how this was the first day we knew the time of

---

2. This would have been his twenty-first birthday.

Pershore
Abbey.

our departure. Each expecting the other to do so, none of us had brought a watch, yet we had got on very well without one. This one fact speaks volumes for this kind of life. Think of it: for nearly a fortnight we had been unable to tell the time except when on occasion we caught sight of some public clock. Still, in all conscience nature provides enough clocks. One gets up on awakening, has dinner when hungry and goes to bed at sunset. It is all so delightfully simple. To be sure, convention gets a jag or two now and then, but what has convention to do with such a life?

Not knowing when another village would be sighted we dropped back to Pershore and laid in further supplies. The Abbey at Pershore is a pleasant fragment of a much greater edifice. The present Abbey is the tower and choir of an extensive building, erected by a King of Mercia in about AD 689. Not being redeemed at the Reformation, the greater part was pulled down and sold piecemeal. The sum of £300 not being raised on the sale of the stone, the surrounding land was also sold, so that nowadays on leaving the East door one is immediately faced with a tall boundary wall.

The most interesting part of our visit was, however, not the stone and mortar, but the verger or caretaker – call him what you will – who came running over from the little chapel of St Andrew to tell us about his charge. He discoursed, very much above our heads, about this archway and that pillar and the thingumabob over there.

'When I lecture...' he began and told us about everything in the Abbey. How he had traced the old Saxon font round the country until he ran it to earth in a garden, disguised as a flowerpot. He was interesting but we preferred the River Avon to his river of eloquence, so leaving him absorbed in a glass window we went into town and returned to the *Hebe* with quantities of plums.

The breeze that had been playing about during the earlier part of the day was increased in force and blowing strongly upstream. Hoisting our sail we went spanking towards Evesham, marking our progress with plum stones.

Very soon we had passed our night's camping place and were inspecting a weir with its lock, which latter had to be considered a total loss.[3] After the inspection we decided the better plan would be to drag the *Hebe* round the lock and not over the weir. Accordingly everything was unloaded and dumped above the lock. Then, with a heave and a run, the *Hebe* came out of the water and lay on top of the bank. Light to handle and fleet in the water, *Hebe* is a somewhat cumbersome proposition on land. Indeed, it required all the strength of the crew to get her on to the upper level.

The whole operation took about thirty minutes and we were very glad to be able to sit back and let the wind rush us along, past the quaint village of Wyre Piddle perched on its high bank. As we went smartly away two young campers running to watch us pass had to race as hard as they could to keep pace with us. Not only was the breeze serving well but the Commander had succeeded in bending a third sail in the shape of an old mizzen which he turned into a foresail.

The country is beautifully wooded and was especially lovely in the warm sunlight. We sailed all morning without having to use the oars and the wind was in the best possible direction for sailing up the Avon. Even round the many twists and turns of the river we always managed to beat our way.

---

3. This was most likely Wyre Lock, 12 miles down from Evesham.

Hebe ashore.

We had an exciting passage at Cropthorne. Through the broken gate of the staunch[4] the river was lashing and foaming with fury at these narrow limits. A score or more of spectators gathered to watch us battle our way through, expecting us to be swept downstream or else have to punt and pole our way up. But wait and hear our story.

The wind stood us in good stead and gradually we got nearer the staunch. With the Mate at the helm and the Commander feeling for the utmost ounce of air, foot by foot and inch by inch we fought our way through the roaring current towards the open gateway, speeding through water but hardly moving in relation to the land. Just as we reached the middle of the gateway our speed slackened, we moved slower, stood still, and then a gust of wind came belting up. We breasted the stream picking up way. Heeling before this new strength, with gunwhale almost awash, *Hebe* seemed to shake herself and in a minute had leapt forward into the calmer water and slid strongly away as though conscious of a mighty victory.

Within five minutes of Cropthorne we came to Fladbury. The lock appeared to be passable but in reality was a hidden death trap. For, as the level of the water within the lock rose, it could be seen that the lower gates, instead of setting back on each other and forming an unbreakable arch, were overlapping and in imminent danger of breaking away.

As we made this discovery a sort of congenital idiot, who had been standing by watching us all the time, informed us that the use of this lock had been forbidden by the River Commissioners.

---

4. A staunch, or flash lock, was one of the earliest forms of navigation consisting of a single gate in the stream holding back the upper part of the river to gain depth. To navigate the gate has to be opened – hard work if you are going up, hairy if you are going down.

Far be it for us to disobey the Commissioners. Anyhow, we did not wish to be involved in any vulgar accident, so hastily emptying the lock we drew out and inspected the land with a view to making another portage. The best place seemed to be at the edge of the weir, and indeed we had just seen two canoes dragged over.

Before attempting the feat of strength of hauling the boat up the thirty feet of very steep incline, we thought it best to have lunch. Halfway through the meal we heard a clock strike the hour. It wasn't lunch it was tea! So we hurriedly put on the kettle, opened a tin of fruit and had two meals in one. This, of course, would not have happened had we been rowing all morning. It just shows what catastrophes can occur even in the best-run boats. Here were we, lots of lovely things in the larder, plenty of time and splendid weather, yet we were actually on the brink of foregoing a meal. Ye Gods and little fishes!

The river above Fladbury is enchanting in all its aspects. In the evening, as we glided silently upstream, the magic of this vale seemed all concentrated around us and we moved in a pleasant dream. Not a ripple to disturb the reflections, not a leaf moving in the woods, no sound from anything, yet we were continually drawn along as though some fairy were with us. The sun was sinking in a glory and enveloped everything with a crimson halo enhancing the glamour of the evening, so almost we slumbered as we sailed.

The rumbling of a weir eventually disturbed us and we knew we had reached Chadbury.[5] We hoped that the lock would be in a workable state and our hopes rose higher when as we approached we saw a derrick alongside it. Sadly there was disappointment when, on inspection, the new gates were seen not in their proper places but floating about inside the lock itself.

The task of making a portage this time did not promise to be so great as on former occasions. The weir was not steep and at one end were rollers fitted for just such times as this. They had, of course, long ago retired from active rolling and could be more accurately described as passive resisters. Their presence, however, did give us considerable help.

Once the heaviest things were unloaded we were able to leave the rest on board for the portage. Though we had rollers it was not too easy a job on account of the slippery weeds, so we were very glad when the *Hebe* was once more afloat.

Three miles from Chadbury and the river is right in the middle of Evesham. It was too late when we arrived to go into the town but we inspected the town weir and the beautiful bridge, every now and then skipping out of the way of fussy pleasure steamers.

---

5. Three miles below Evesham.

Fladbury Lock and Weir, from a contemporary postcard.

Evesham from the river.

We could not decide where to camp but eventually determined on a spot about two miles downstream. With both of us at the oars we made for it, putting all our strength into sending the boat flying along. Such good time did we make that numerous townsfolk taking their evening walk on the esplanade raised a great cheer as we flashed by in the gloaming.

WEDNESDAY 13TH AUGUST

The next day dawned bright and very sunny. At six p.m. we were to meet two other members of the crew who had missed the boat at High Lane and had arranged to meet us in Evesham.

Having plenty of time in hand, therefore, we made the day one of spit and polish, an irregular thing to do on a Wednesday and contrary to all sea lore. Nevertheless we dared to do it. With great dashings and splashings and rubbings and scrubbings the *Hebe* gradually regained something of her pristine glory. The river, it is true, became sadly tinged with the dust of Birmingham, the red muds of the Severn and the loam of Warwickshire, but what a magnificent result was obtained in the end.

Every inch of varnish sparkling like the sun, cargo stowed in shipshape fashion and the coconut matting washed and dried was almost white. Odd tins of fruit and soap disappeared into their respective boxes and, as a grand finale, all ropes coiled in a manner calculated to put envy into the heart of the oldest of tars.

At length, towards five o'clock (we learned the time from a handy fisherman), carefully and delicately casting off, we made our way up to Evesham. We had arranged to meet the others – the Commodore and the Engineer – below the bridge at about six pm; however a letter at the Post Office from the Commodore informed us that they would arrive at the station at about nine o'clock. We left the *Hebe* in the charge of a friendly boat hirer and walked off on a short sightseeing tour until eight-fifteen when we went to the station to meet their train. They were not on the train arranged, neither were they on the last train which came in at about half-past nine. Then, going back to the *Hebe*, who should we meet but the two missing crew, arrived in Evesham some hours before on some unheard of train. It is worth noting that although *Hebe* was well under the bridge they had located her – by her conspicuous smartness, declared the Commodore.

It was now getting dark so we pulled away upstream to the lock island, where not only was the cover stretched over the *Hebe* but the up to now unused tent was erected, in which Commander and Mate laid themselves, giving up their comfortable couches on board saying they were well hardened to anything.

Evesham Weir.

THURSDAY 14TH AUGUST

Thursday continued the run of glorious weather that had prevailed from the beginning of the trip. After a grand bathe and breakfast a splendid breeze invited us to go upstream and this was a chance not to be missed, so we decided during the marmalade to try the waters of the Upper Avon.

Just then a voice hailed us from a houseboat moored in midstream just below the lock. It appeared the young man calling us had two friends. Rising bright and early these companions had not only secreted his 'bags'[6] but also went off in the only moveable boat they had.

So here was our friend (having by this time recovered his 'bags') marooned in mid-stream and extremely anxious to get to his office. Would we, as we had a boat, be so good out of the kindness of our hearts to ferry this lost mariner to land. We were happy to oblige and soon a very thankful young man was jumping ashore from the *Hebe*.

After this we soon packed up and started away. Immediately we came to the weir. The lock was out of order,[7] but there were rollers and with four

---

6. Trousers?
7. *Bradshaw's Guide* (1904) notes: 'The Upper Avon navigation from Evesham to Stratford on Avon fell into decay and ceased to be navigable about the year 1873.'

strong men the *Hebe* almost took them in one bound and in three minutes was floating serenely on the Upper Avon. The wind was serving well and in a very short while we were tearing upstream at a good ten knots.

The Upper Avon is shallow and infested with shoals, but a good lookout and tricky steering succeeded in keeping us clear of rocks and sandbars for the most part. In one or two places, however, with the river surging and swirling around us we were alarmed to feel a scrape on the bottom and a great heave as we bumped onto a sandbar. Luckily in each case our great speed carried us on into deeper water and no harm was done.

After about an hour's fast sailing with the stream getting alarmingly shallow, we began to look out for the old Harvington lock. When we sighted the 'Anchor' the lock had apparently been removed. All we could find was a ford across the river, over which water was pouring like round green stones. The Commander remembered there used to be a lock here but none of the natives could. An old cowherd was the only person we could find who knew anything about it. Mine host of the 'Anchor' had never even heard of it. However, by carefully examining the river bed we could make out the foundations of the old lock walls.

Deciding that it was time to turn our prow homewards we skillfully executed this manoeuvre and were rapidly borne away on the fast stream.

Chapter V

Turning Homewards

The swift-running current now rushed us downstream almost as fast as the wind had borne us up. Soon we were at Evesham, and of course had to use the rollers, but now the *Hebe* needed very little persuasion to move. Indeed, on the downward slope she almost had to be held back.

It was the same at Chadbury. Here, however, the passage over the rollers was not so comfortable because of the way the water was running about them. At Evesham the roller ramp was bone dry. Here it was not.

In the evening when we came to Fladbury Mill it presented a sight which could not be improved one iota. Regard the photo for a moment. The upper river was a broad stretch of amazingly calm water. The woods on the bank were dark and sombre, yet the rays of the setting sun lit up the warm red brick of the mill with a note of heavenly fire. The leaves of the creeper caught the sun and reflected it with a hundred different patterns, and in the foam of the weir baby rainbows flashed about. No words of mine can adequately describe such a revelation; it had something in it too magnificent for mere words. Only Constable's brush could do it justice in any way. Regretful at having to say farewell to such a picturesque scene, we pulled away in the direction of Pershore.

Almost before we realised it we had come to the town of plums and were gliding past the Angel gardens. Below the lock, as we raced on the stream which had tried our skill on the way up, we found a score or so of motorboats, each one ablaze with lights. We passed by them in disdain and scorn. In spite of their superior airs they were now unable to go any further, while the *Hebe* could wander into the quiet spots of which they had never heard. Imagine trying to haul one of these craft over a weir.

Daylight was far gone when we finally got clear of this society and were forced to camp in a not altogether suitable spot. At least it was unsuitable for the Commander and the Mate; the other two slept on board and were

Two views of Fladbury Mill.
Above: on the *Hebe* trip.
Below: forty-four years later, after the
navigation was restored (see Plate 13).

Another view of Fladbury Mill.

as comfortable as ever. Our tent had to be pitched at the top of a very steep bank in a bed of nettles. Surprisingly, only two stings resulted from sleeping in such risky quarters.

FRIDAY 15TH AUGUST

Although the camping place was over a mile from Pershore, the Commander and the Engineer decided to go into the town for shopping, leaving the other two to engage in that process known to the rest of the world as shaving. It was nearly midday when the expedition returned laden with quantities of produce. For instance, plums sold at a penny a pound. This cargo having been safely stowed, we made haste to start.

We were making such speed with two rowers all the time that at one point the Engineer (who occasionally forgets he has an oar in each hand) succeeded in breaking a rowlock.

During dinner, taken in the depth of a thick wood, we were astonished to see the water rising six or seven inches. 'Aha,' said we, 'tumult in the north.'

The afternoon was very sunny and although, with the broken rowlock, only two oars were available, we managed to make Strensham before tea time. Little time was lost in passing this lock as on this occasion there was no motor boat to care for.

In the evening we slowly drifted downstream past Bredon and Twyning, finally coming to rest comparatively early in a willow copse above Tewkesbury. Leaving *Hebe* under the care of the Commander, the rest of the crew set off in the direction of the town. The object of this expedition was to investigate the daily outgoings of trains from Tewkesbury, for alas the Mate was to leave us the next day. By the time the station was found all was silent as the grave and little or no satisfaction could be gained.

However, the visit to the town was successful in one way – we were able to increase the Commander's stock of tobacco. He insists on smoking the most obscure brands, and when on a voyage all shoppers are required to look out for them. The trouble is getting the right kind. In general, after searching half the tobacconists in the town we are fobbed off with some other 'recommended' brand which is added to the Commander's store until the day comes when he has none of his regular brand and has to resort to one of these strangers. With great reminiscences he will search through his store, rejecting this one from Worcester or that one from Gloucester and finally selecting the other from goodness knows where.

SATURDAY 16TH AUGUST

When we woke there was a mist over the country auguring well for the weather. Before breakfast we rowed upstream to the bathing pool for a swim, and while we were in the water the sun came out. In a moment the mist was licked up, the air becoming as clear as crystal, and we were able to see the airship R101 returning from her visit to America.[1]

A considerable diversion was created during the latter part of breakfast by a troop of Boy Scouts and Wolf Cubs who came down to swim.

Having got everything ready, and with the Mate in all the glory of a complete suit and tie, we rowed down to Tewkesbury and reached

---

1. The airship R101 was built by the government in direct parallel with the privately built R100 (on which both Barnes Wallis and Neville Shute worked). On 5 October 1930, on an intended voyage to Karachi designed to open up the India route, it crashed near Beauvais, France, with the loss of forty-eight lives, including Lord Thompson, Secretary of State for Air. The crash effectively ended all British involvement with rigid airships.

The *Hebe* in sail on the Avon. There was virtually no image left on the original print and no negative was available. The quality is therefore not good, but it is included because it is one of the few reasonably close pictures of the *Hebe* when rigged.

Bathurst's at about eleven o'clock. Almost an hour passed while the Mate and the Engineer went off to find when the trains left; the other two stayed with the boat and supervised the repair of the broken rowlock.

The all-important train did not leave before a quarter to two and when various purchases had been made there arose the question of lunch – whether to go upstream and make our own or to visit some hostelry. In his many wanderings about the town the Commander's observant eye had picked out the Black Bear. It, he said, held the possibility of lunch, so accordingly we adjourned to the dining room of the Black Bear to investigate the quality of their lamb and mint sauce.

We recommend this inn to all and sundry. Tewkesbury was very hot and dusty and the streets were blocked by long-distance buses. Our dining room, formerly used as a stable and from about 1482, was a dim, cool habour of refuge. The lamb and mint sauce were beyond reproach, the French beans as tender as could be and the potatoes miracles of floweriness. What a lunch we had, washed down with glorious Worcestershire cider. The Mate, poor man, was forced to leave us before the cheese, and bidding a long farewell rushed off for his train.

A Severn tug. While ADS processed many of his own photographs, he was not always careful with the results. This one in particular shows fingerprints all over it! The cost of materials and chemicals would have been fairly high so he probably made do with just one print.

The Engineer was now agog to reach the Severn, of whose vastness he had heard so much. In the afternoon, therefore, we dropped through the last lock on the Avon and a hundred strokes brought us to fair Sabrina.

A gentle zephyr was making up from the sea so we hoisted sail, only to discover that gentle zephyrs are hardly a match for the Severn's current. On we went past the delicate arch of the Mythe bridge, gradually forging upstream, the Engineer making a comical sight as for the sake of the ultra-violet rays doffed his shirt, but for the sake of decency donned it again every time a motor boat came past, even though he was wearing a hat all the time.

In the evening we succeeded in reaching Upton on Severn. It was so crowded and dusty in the town that we fled with relief to the river and the pleasant air of the *Hebe*. Then, as it grew darker, we began to look out for a suitable camping ground.

'Oh, I know a lovely place, just right,' said the Commander. 'The Mate and I stopped there on the way out. It is the mouth of the Teme and surely is not far distant.'

We kept a good watch, the Commander being certain the Teme was nearby, but as we went on and on and rounded corner after corner, the Teme seemed further and further away. In the end it got so dark we gave up the search and moored for the night on a quiet bend in the stream.

Mythe Bridge.

SUNDAY 17TH AUGUST

To say the least, our start in the morning was on the late side. We did not get away until nearly noon. A curious fishing competition was taking place on the opposite bank, the object of it seemed to be not how many fish could be caught but how many times the bait could be drawn out of the water. Towards one o'clock we came to the River Teme, the spot which the Commander had had in mind the night before.

We could not pass without visiting it and so went into the Teme for lunch. While the water for peas was boiling we stripped and plunged into the river, disturbing a couple of swans who had followed us in expectation of sharing our meal.

The Teme is a fascinating stream. It is very narrow with high banks lined with willows which project over the water as they age and then tumble in – a menace to boats but a great hiding place for fishes. The water is like plate glass, crystal clear yet with that greenish hue common in good glass. Rising from the eastern slopes of Plinlimmon in the Welsh mountains, not twenty miles from the sources of both the Severn and Wye, it wanders in a picturesque course through the counties of Hereford and Worcester to its confluence with the Severn below Diglis.

Leaving the Teme after lunch we were soon through Diglis lock and nearing Worcester, that stronghold of Royalists. The cathedral, built in the thirteenth century, was, after the Reformation, gradually allowed to fall into decay until 1847 when it was restored. After the cathedral, Worcester is famous for its fine

River wildlife,
from a glass
positive (i.e.
reversal) which
ADS probably
used as a magic
lantern slide.

pottery and porcelain works, lately just escaped bankruptcy. We made a short visit to the town but were glad to get away again.

The Boat Club was looking very fine in the summer sun, with so many white flannels and pretty dresses about it. Soon after leaving Worcester we began to look out for a place for tea. It was difficult to find a spot where the banks are less than fifteen feet high or which was not already occupied by a boating party, for the citizens of Worcester made good use of their river. In the end we moored at a corner and had tea on board.

Several times during the meal we had to fend off from the bank so that the wash from pleasure steamers might not swamp us, the Commander meanwhile relating stories of how people had drowned in exactly similar circumstances.

The peace of the afternoon was disturbed by one of these motor boats which appeared on the scene with a noise like a Lewis Gun and trailing two fishing rods. As is nearly always the case the motor was not on its best behaviour and a little while after leaving our sight we saw it drifting helplessly downstream, a fierce quarrel going on between the crew as to the exact nature of the motor lesion. Eventually they got beyond our sight and we know not what befell them.

In the evening we made our way up above Holt Lock, near Hampstall ferry. We stopped early that night so as to be not far from Worcester.

MONDAY 18TH AUGUST

The Commander and Engineer, as ever, set off in the morning to pay a visit to Worcester. They naturally missed the one and only 'bus from Holt but caught another an hour later some two miles away. It was ten-thirty before they really started on their way and as the ancient vehicle lumbered along it gradually accumulated a varied assortment of passengers. One of these, a female of the species, caught our attention. Tall and angular, she was dressed in a blue costume which showed off to a nicety the redness of her hair and the emerald green of her hat. She stood in the middle of the road gesticulating to our driver, a remarkable figure, for which later we were to be quite thankful.

In the course of time we reached the city. It was crowded, so making purchases and ascertaining no letters were waiting, the expedition made haste to return. The 'bus stand was crowded with 'buses. How to identify our particular one? Like most country 'buses they had no destination boards and were all pretty much alike. Ah! What is that? Red hair and green hat? The very same! Here is our vehicle. Another forty minutes and we were rowing away from Hampstall towards Stourport. Four or five miles and we needed lunch so a grassy bank by a cliff was selected and we set in.

We were fortunate in choosing this spot for (we liked to imagine) here we saved a life. Two fishermen were on the bank and one had just tumbled into the river and was shivering and shaking. Quickly we had the kettle boiling and filled him with hot tea, thus warding off pneumonia or some other fatal condition.

In the afternoon we passed Lincomb Lock and were in Stourport about four o'clock. On the way out, while we were still on the Stafford and Worcester Canal, the Commander had noted a lock from the canal onto the River Stour. He now suggested it would be very pleasant to enter the canal from this stream.

When we were opposite the confluence we turned in and soon found we had got into what was a very narrow trickle, more of a drain. Nevertheless the Commander still maintained there was a way into the canal so we endeavoured to carry on between concrete walls and behind factories in the hope of a sudden widening.

The conditions became too severe even for us, so we had to go astern and return to the Severn to enter the canal in the orthodox manner through the docks. There we passed a curious cargo, a boatload of sugar bound for Bournville.

Now we were back on the canal system again and what a contrast to the Severn. One thing helped us to bear the change, however, for in the canal we were no longer rowing against a strong current.

The Further Adventures of the Hebe (1930)

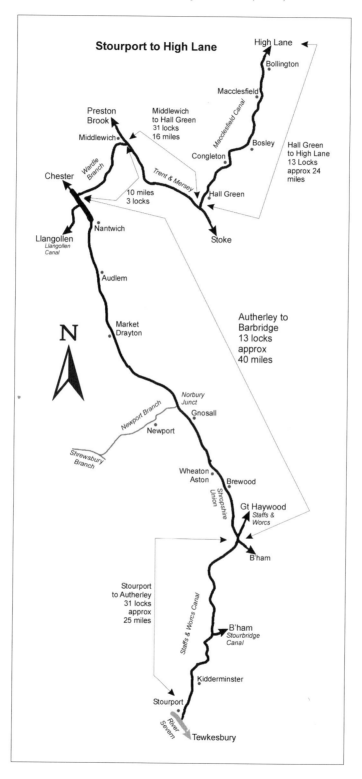

The caves near Stourport.

Once outside Stourport a shower threatened us, so gaining a woody bank we kept dry and made some tea. The shower soon passed and left us free to proceed when presently the mystery of the lock onto the Stour was made clear. To begin with the lock really did exist. It was there alright and what is more there were barges in the river. Where did this navigation go? An old rustic supplied the all-important information: the River Stour was navigable for only a few hundred yards. It had been canalised in order that coal might be carried to Mr Baldwin's ironworks.[2]

As the evening drew on and the sun went down we found ourselves approaching Kidderminster just when we should have been nearing open country. So putting our weight into it we fairly flew along, to the great delight of the local populace who were hard put to keep up with us.

When the stars were beginning to show themselves properly we found a little offshoot of the canal, remnant of a former dock now sadly overgrown. This seemed an ideal place for the night and we hurried to snug down.

---

2. The junction with the River Stour was through Pratt's Wharf Lock between locks 3 and 4, a little over 2 miles above Stourport.

Just as we were preparing for sleep there came a rush of hooves along the towpath, then a sudden shouting and flow of eloquence: 'Look out Sam, 'ere, a ★★★★★★★ canoe!'

Investigation showed that a late barge was endeavouring to turn round in the dock and was somewhat startled by our presence. A very few words and all was peace, the boatman explaining that it was the shock of seeing us which had upset him, and promising that not only would his boat not touch us but also that there would be no further disturbances that night.

TUESDAY 19TH AUGUST

In the light of day when we arose our camping ground was seen to be a most picturesque spot. In olden days this dock must have been very busy, serving a small carpet factory of which very little was left. The old mill pond still existed and drove a water wheel turning a machine for making stuffing for upholstery. An old gaffer longing for conversation turned up before we were away and was delighted to show the Commander the way to the pump.

'That's the best water in Staffordshire. Like wine, as the saying is.'

Besides this he insisted on the Commander taking a great basin of beans from his garden.

'Dinna take th'owd 'uns,' he said in his genial way. 'Take young 'uns, they'm nicer.'

Just as, full of thanks to our friend, we were about to take off, the owner of the water wheel turned up anxious that it should be photographed.

'That theer wheel's bin goin' round nigh on a hundred year.'

We had not gone far before reaching the village of Kinver. Here supplies were laid in and afterwards we lunched at the edge of a great field of flowers. The charming villages we were passing all rejoiced in the quaintest of names. What could be more delightful than to live in a hamlet called Wolverley Court, Kingswinford, Gornal Wood or Stewponey. There is something tremendously suggestive of domestic peace about such names and one cannot help contemplating with fine feeling sounds like those of Wandersley, Enville or Brierly Hill.

We had hoped to find ourselves above the Bratch before settling down but darkness overtook us while still some distance away and we moored by a low-lying field which presented itself readily enough.

We were not alone that night. Towards ten o'clock two campers returned to their nearby tent and proceeded to light a fire and cook their supper.

'Bin goin' round for nigh on a hundred year.' A waterwheel, from an original glass negative. For waterwheel buffs this looks roughly 9 feet in diameter and about 8 feet wide. It is clearly a breast-shot wheel, which is not the most efficient type, in reasonably good condition.

WEDNESDAY 20TH AUGUST

The day came with all the sun which had been characteristic of the weather until now. With an urge to get on we were away by eight-thirty. Half an hour later we were once more approaching the Bratch. Our old friend the lock keeper was waiting to receive us with open arms. He greeted us in a most jovial manner and helped us with the gates, pleasure written all over his ruddy countenance. From the way he filled our water cans you would have thought we were royalty.

We seemed this morning destined to meet old acquaintances. As we passed the next lock who should we meet but the barge navigated by the boys who had proved so useful when we were coming down the Wolverhampton locks.

The wind was in our favour so that all morning we sailed happily from lock to lock, every now and then lowering our flag to calm the fears of some excited barge horse. After lunch we found ourselves on the outskirts of Tettenhall and here the Post Office was suspected of harbouring our letters. Accordingly, while the Commander pretended to mind the *Hebe*, the other members of the crew went in search of correspondence. Three Post Offices in the vicinity of the canal were searched in vain. There remained but one hope – Upper Tettenhall Office itself. This was at least a mile away, all the time the sun was beating down in a royal way, and we had already walked a considerable distance. Nevertheless, with some hope, off we went towards the great hill at the top of which was our destination. At last we arrived but horrors! Anarchy! Larceny! And other things. It was Wednesday and the Office was shut!

We could not face the walk back and so looked around for some conveyance. Presently a great juggernaut rolled along, and resisting the temptation to throw ourselves under it we boarded and were swiftly borne away.

The Engineer, ignorant of the colossal fares charged on these vehicles, tendered what he thought might be a fair and correct sum. The conductor looked at it, contemplated the Engineer's shorts, open shirt and hatless head and inquired in a puzzled voice as if ready to be corrected, 'You're over fourteen, aren't you?' This Napoleon having received an affirmative answer then demanded further largesse. In high dudgeon we prepared to dismount, luckily finding ourselves at the canal side.

The wind was still more in our favour once we rounded Autherley. At the stop lock we were surprised to find moored a pleasure boat. It was motor-driven, its crew (all dressed most nautically) informed us with great pride that they had come through thirty locks and done sixty miles since last Saturday, which was four days ago. We congratulated them and told how the *Hebe* had once done nearly sixty miles in a day's sailing, and that upstream.

That night we had only just snuggled in near Wheaton Aston when the rain came pelting down. Darkness had fallen in earnest and all was quiet except for the unceasing drip among the trees. Then faintly, but ever increasing, there came to our ears the heavy chug chug of a motor barge. Our lamp was lit so that we were quite visible, and it was just as well because we were drawn close to a bridge and this boat would pass very near. However, as he passed, in response to our shouted inquiry he let us know that several more motors would be coming that night and we were in danger of being bumped.

The Commander was accordingly sent out into the rain and wet grass with lantern and double mooring lines. After much struggling he got us back into a safer place under a protecting hedge and here we slept comfortably all night with not a single boat passing by.[3]

---

3. At this point in the story my father added some extra notes: 'At Norbury Junction we turned for Shrewsbury and eventually forced our way to that town, being, I think, the last boat to go there.' He took several pictures of this venture (all on glass plate negatives).

Lock No. 2 on the Newport Branch. It is a guillotine lock and my grandfather is standing by the gate paddle. This canal was officially abandoned in 1944.

Above: Berwick Tunnel (970 yards), about 5 miles from Shrewsbury. *Bradshaw's Guide* states: 'There is a white mark in the middle of the tunnel. Should two boats meet the one who has reached the middle of the tunnel first has right of way.' The width is given as 7 feet!

Right: Forcing a way into Shrewsbury. This is the only picture later annotated: 'R W Rattray (d'cd 1980) steering, Lloyd Galloway holding the ? towing mast.'

Aboard the *Hebe*. My father is on the left with the steering ropes in hand. The second man is unidentified.

THURSDAY 21ST AUGUST

Dull and wet. The same weather as the night before. We waited some time and eventually the rain stopped and a watery sun came out. The country through which we were now passing was interesting in an agricultural sort of way, quite typical of Shropshire and rustic Cheshire.

At Tyrley we passed through the tremendous cutting hewn through the rock, its walls rising to a lofty height all clothed in greenery and shining wet in the sun. The width of water is just sufficient to allow boats to pass and no more, consequently when half a dozen barges came along we had an anxious moment or two. However, we reached Tyrley locks without mishap and found ourselves in open country again.

All day we continued, floating placidly along through Shropshire and into Cheshire with the Wrekin and Brown Clee away to port, and the country stretching flat to Cannock Chase on our starboard bow. At Audlem locks there was some slight misunderstanding with a barge. We never quite got to the root of the matter and all passed off without blows on either side, but a state of frigidity continued to exist between us.

Audlem locks.

Cowley Tunnel, from a commercial print.

It must have been eight o'clock when we cleared the last of the fifteen Audlem locks and we had not gone a hundred yards before a gale of wind sprang up blowing in the right direction. Breaking out sail we fled onwards through the gathering gloom at a rate of knots. The banks surged past, the broken water sang and gurgled under our lee while gradually the light faded and velvet darkness spread over the land.

Finally, as our nerves were about to give way with the frenzied excitement of continually passing almost unseen bridges, the magical wind dropped and we camped for the night.

FRIDAY 22ND AUGUST

The same wind that had served so well the night before now came in the morning with added force, blowing away the mists and vapours of the night, singing madly in the wires and letting the sun shine strongly.

Nothing loth, we hoisted sail and soon were slipping through the water like some sprite. The banks glided calmly by, the water rippled under the bow and washed gleefully ashore, cordage creaked as an extra capful of wind caught our sails, sleek horses whinnied and neighed as they caught sight of us, and all the time milestones flew by with ease, the only interruptions being when a bridge required the temporary lowering of sail.

Thus we flew all morning. By the time we were hungry enough to stop for lunch we had rounded the corner at Barbridge and were some distance towards Middlewich. Before having lunch we carefully weighed the penalties of bathing in the canal against the pleasures gained from such an activity. Then in spite of the warning notices we plunged in for a glorious swim.

In the evening we reached Middlewich when the majority of the population was apparently taking a constitutional along the canal bank. Our passage thus caused considerable tumult. Not that this is in any way extraordinary, but in this case the commotion was so great as to give us cause to fear that the foremost ranks of the large crowd would be precipitated into the water by pressure behind.

However, by dint of shouted warnings we managed to prevent any fatal accident. A couple of hundred youths came pelting after us as we left the lock but we put on pace so that a bare half dozen survived the eight hundred yards to the next lock.

Here we met an old and venerable friend of the Commander's in the shape of the lock keeper. There were warm greetings all round and reminiscences of former voyages. What astonishment at this one. How tall the Mate had

Above and below: Hebe in locations unknown.

grown since his first voyage. How well the old man was looking and what a pity all his teeth had come out. Geniality reigned supreme as we were locked through.

The evening was now growing darker and soon we were looking out for the usual mooring point – no small difficulty in a narrow canal where a great deal of traffic is continually passing. An excellent harbour was found in the tail-race of a corn mill. Here we were quite safe, and soon, supper finished, we dropped off to sleep.

SATURDAY 23RD AUGUST

When we left Tewkesbury we had started out on a long uphill staircase. We had gone always higher as we came through the valley of the Stour until we came to the high level at Autherley. From there we dropped down and down onto the Cheshire plain and now, leaving Middlewich, we were to go sharply up again by a great flight of locks almost to the level of the Harecastle Tunnel which pierces the last hill of the Pennines. Thus today was to be a day of locks. Up and up and still higher we were to go. There are thirty-one locks between Middlewich and Hardings Wood and we had to pass them all. Up in good time we found the weather damp and dismal. This delayed our start for a while but we eventually got under way in good order.

Now a lock is often an interesting thing. Far from being the terror which many people imagine, a lock is usually quite a welcome diversion. Nevertheless, a flight of thirty-one is too much of a good thing. Dogged does it, as Socrates said (if not he should have done), and steadily we put lock after lock astern.

Towards two o'clock in a blink of wet weather we reached Poole's Lock and took shelter under the aqueduct over which we would soon go[4] while the Commander bargained for stores. The next lock but one, in the middle of a gas works, was under the charge of another old friend of the *Hebe's*. He related how he had piloted a motor boat up these very locks and around into *Hebe's* home waters a few days before; with many chuckles he told how first the engine would refuse or else the propeller would get caught up with weeds.

'Last I heard on 'em was the' were at Congleton Thursday, it were Wednesday as I left 'em and it's only about eight mile fra' here.'

---

4. I think he means Red Bull Lock (No. 43). The Macclesfield Canal loops round and over the Trent and Mersey on Poole Aqueduct and joins it two locks above this one at Hardings Wood Junction.

Leaving him waving to us, a few good strokes brought us into the Macclesfield canal. We were almost at home.

Like some hysterical female the sky wept copiously upon us. A bridge was handy – indeed a bridge is always handy in these waters – under which we stopped, and while lightning flashed and thunder growled we took a meal, either dinner or tea, we were not quite sure. A couple of hours and all was over so we hurried on through a steaming wet countryside.

The Engineer was anxious to reach the village of Congleton where he hoped to collect several letters. Great haste was necessary as it was now six-thirty and the Post Office would close at eight o'clock. There were still seven miles to go. In spite of all our efforts it was a quarter past eight when we got there and the Office was shut like a tomb. By half past eight we were going on through inky darkness, an unusual thing for us but somehow we were determined to reach Bosley that night.

It is a curious experience dashing along at night. Like a dream we knew we were moving through the water, not seeing the towing figure ahead and only occasionally hearing a splash as he startled a vole or his hollow footsteps as he passed under a bridge. Again, bridges were felt rather than seen, only the blackness seemed a degree darker and the air a bit colder as we passed through. The actual shape and position of the structure was impossible to make out. At last when we heard the River Dane booming under its aqueduct we knew we had reached our destination and camped for the night.

SUNDAY 24TH AUGUST

It was an undiplomatic stroke to camp below the locks. When we approached the second lock on the Sunday morning it was to find both it and the third lock under repair and unworkable. What made it worse was that the repairs had only started at six o'clock that morning – last night they were still in order.

The prospect of a long portage up a steep hill under blazing August sun did not appeal but we had to do it. We managed, however, to save ourselves a lot of trouble by borrowing a wheelbarrow. Three journeys with this and all our luggage was above the stoppage, there only remained the boat itself.

It was the simple matter of a few seconds to run her out of the water but this was only the preliminary round. First the boat was turned over and her stern was placed on the barrow. A stout stick was put across under the bows and we were ready. With the Commander wheeling the barrow, and the other two lifting the bows with the stick, off we went.

Home waters.

Slowly and cautiously, fearing to strain the delicate structure, we pushed and pulled up the towpath. What a relief when we at last got to the top and were able to get the boat onto the water. After a short rest we loaded up and before midday had left the top lock behind us and had settled down for a sail. The wind was not great but we deserved a respite, especially if we could also maintain our progress.

Gradually we came upon more and more familiar scenes as we drew nearer and nearer to High Lane. Here was Macclesfield, the cradle of the silk industry. Here was Poynton where they loaded fireclay for smoky Dukinfield. How delightful it was to point out old landmarks to each other even though the *Hebe* had been away for only a month.

At Poynton was our old friend the banksman who was coming along the towpath, as glad to see us as we him, although to be sure we never exchange more than a dozen words.

Finally, as the sun set in a blaze of glory somehow befitting the end of such an adventure, the *Hebe* slid quietly into her boathouse, the doors were locked and we returned to civilisation.[5]

---

5. As far as I am able to judge, this trip lasted 25 days and covered 269 locks and approximately 346 miles.

APPENDICES

THE UPS AND DOWNS OF THE HEBE

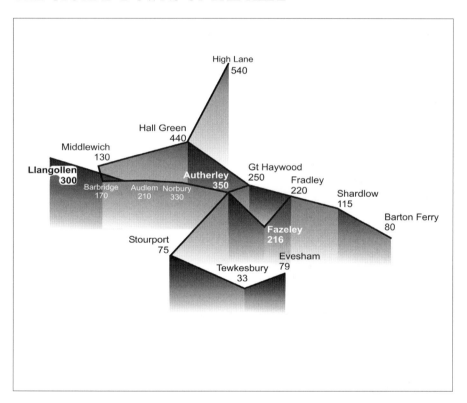

A representation of the various levels attained by the *Hebe* during the adventures featured in this book. The figures are approximate heights (in feet) above sea level (see Plate 14).

THE MAN

The author of these three Adventures was my father, Arthur Desmond Stoker (ADS). He was born on 12 August 1909 at Huyton, Liverpool, and educated at Stockport Grammar School and also at Rydal in North Wales.

He was a medical student at Edinburgh University during these Adventures – only three were written up but there must have been many others – and graduated MB ChB in 1933. After a couple of other posts he went to Nottingham General Hospital as a Casualty Officer (where he met my mother, who was a physiotherapist there) and then, in 1935, took up practice as a GP in Winster, Derbyshire. He married in 1936.

Commissioned into the TA RAMC, he was called up in 1939 and posted to the Far East, seeing service in Iraq and India before being posted to Burma, where he landed on 8 December 1941, the day after the Japanese attack on Pearl Harbour.

He served with 57 Indian Field Ambulance until the Battle of Yennangyaung and then took charge of an Irrawaddy Steamer being used as a hospital ship. This was worked up to Katha where patients and such staff who had not already deserted were transferred to a railway engine and five trucks. They drove this train to the rail head at Myitkyina, where most of the wounded

Desmond and Simon Stoker assisting the Duchess of Devonshire in christening a new passenger boat on the Cromford Canal.

'Pop'. My grandfather, Stephen Stoker, with pipe and oar.

were evacuated, leaving him and some others to walk out of Burma by the long route of the Hukawng Valley (not the easy 'Burma Road' taken by the bulk of the Army), some 400 miles through the jungle to India. He was most likely one of the last Medical Officers to escape the Japanese.

Resuming his practice in 1946, he was the local doctor for nearly fifty years and was proud of the continuity which allowed him to have, at one time, four or five generations of the same family as his patients.

Always a keen canal traveller, he owned consecutively three narrowboats and a 'cruiser'. The first two were converted to his specification and the cruiser was built to his design by Tom Trevethick's yard in Lenton, Nottingham. As a family we must have covered many hundreds of miles and even more locks around the English canal system in the various boats.

In the late 1960s he became actively involved in the restoration of the Cromford Canal[1] in Derbyshire, becoming the project's chairman for many years. The operation ran horse-drawn passenger boats (I wonder where he got the idea!) and also restored the massive Leawood Beam Engine used to pump water to the canal.

He died in 1993 at the age of eighty-four. These Adventures are part of a great legacy.

---

1. The full story of the Cromford work is told in Simon Stoker, *There and Back Again: Restoring the Cromford Canal, 1968–88* (Amberley, 2008).

THE BOAT

Hebe with its covers raised.

Hebe's sail rig.

An image of the *Hebe* on the Macclesfield Canal during an adventure that doesn't appear in the original books. ADS is behind on the left. Given that he is in the picture, it may have been taken by his brother. The girls are unidentified.

Hebe on horseback – a striking image of ADS (far left) and his beloved boat during a portage on another unchronicled adventure.

Monday 12th August.

The sun was shining gloriously from a cloudless sky, and, helped by a pleasant breeze soon had the dew dried from the cover. But just as we were thinking how dry it was, the same pleasant breeze in its playful little way, got under the cover and lifting it up deposited it in the water. No harm was done, but the cover was quite damp and had to be spread out to dry.

While this process was going on, we were joined by the owner of the neighbouring fields, a farmer ready and eager for conversation. He gave us long dissertations upon railways, and roads, and even the latest cotton prices. He had taken to the wrong calling. The man should have lived in Manchester, and sold stocks, dealt in shares, or, as an agreeable change floated companies, instead of rusticating on a farm in the heart of rural Cheshire.

The would be financier gone, and the cover dry we made haste to pack up and get away. The wind was fairly strong and being against us the Mate elected to row.

The country through which we were passing was that luscious, luxuriant green, characteristic of Cheshire, and with a bright sun and a blue sky flecked with great white cumuli the landscape was perfect.

A page from the original manuscript, which was handwritten with photographs pasted in (see Plate 15).

THE BOOK

Always a keen photographer, and in later life something of a raconteur, my father wrote his little collection of stories only for his own and his family's amusement. Yet they have a broader appeal as an interesting reflection of interwar life. Rather than rely solely on souvenir tickets or postcards to document his adventures, he took a host of pictures that remain valuable as a historical record.

He processed his own black and white photographs, some of them on glass negatives which he took (he once told me) with a Sanderson 'Hand and Stand' camera. I am not sure what other cameras he used. He may well have been in some competition with his elder brother, Brandon, who was also a keen photographer and an Edinburgh-trained GP.

As a darkroom nut myself, I can see that some of his processing was a bit sloppy – the cost would have been a major factor – and some of the prints have faded badly due to poor fixing. However, in the intervening eighty years those clever computer people have provided excellent software capable not only of scanning the originals but also of cleaning them up. As a result I have been able to 'rescue' some images which were virtually lost to the naked eye. For comparison, I have added some later transparencies that my father took on his Roliflex when we re-created (although I did not realise at the time) some of the trips recorded here.

Index

Page references in italics indicate illustrations